COMPLETE GUIDE
TO WINNING
SLOT-I FOOTBALL

by

KEN LYONS

PARKER PUBLISHING COMPANY, INC.

West Nyack, New York

© 1981, *by*

PARKER PUBLISHING COMPANY, INC.

West Nyack, N.Y.

Library of Congress Cataloging in Publication Data

Lyons, Ken
    Complete guide to winning slot-I football.

    Includes index.
1. Football–Offense. 2. Football coaching.
I. Title
GV951.8.L9   796.332'2   81-1534
ISBN 0-13-160697-2   AACR2

No army can withstand the strength of an idea whose time has come.

—Victor Hugo

DEDICATION

This text is dedicated to my parents, the late Mamie and Louis T. Lyons, who were the guiding hand in my life, and to my wife Brenda, who provided the persistent encouragement to complete this project.

ACKNOWLEDGMENT

I wish to extend my appreciative "thanks" to the football coaches who trained me and to the many football players, assistant coaches and fine administrators who made it possible for my football coaching aspirations to become a reality—and made this writing venture possible.

Special acknowledgment is extended to my former assistant David Jakes, who made contributions in research during the early stage of this manuscript, and to the late Mrs. Georgeanne Magee, who provided the proof-reading assistance in my final draft.

MAKING THE MOST OF YOUR OFFENSE

This book on Slot-I football shows you how to put together a highly efficient and explosive run-pass offense. The first chapter presents the evolution of the Slot-I, and clearly explains how the Slot-I became a composite of many other proven systems.

From that point, I will demonstrate how to develop objectives for your offense, define your offensive purpose and implement procedures with this plan. Then I will spell out a simplified method of teaching blocking techniques and of formulating blocking rules and patterns.

Next we approach the ways and means of putting the Slot-I offense into operation, and, as a prerequisite to the play format, a point-blank coverage of coaching pointers is given for backs and receivers. Finally, we begin moving into the heart of the offense in Chapter 8, the "keystone" concept of attack, which gives you the basis for a total, yet simple, attack. Chapter 9 broadens the keystone attack with enrichment plays, while Chapter 10 illustrates how a veer backfield can be combined with the Slot-I as part of its variation package, to intimidate the defense with an expansion of the option and passing game.

I began writing this book with the purpose of solving the complex offensive riddle of matching balance and simplicity with completeness and diversity, while eliminating formation tendencies. In my previous years of coaching, before the versatile Slot-I was implemented, offensive football always seemed to be more-or-less a jigsaw puzzle. The pro-style approach of using a different offensive plan from week to week never seemed to give satisfactory results. In a relentless search for the bits and pieces necessary to discover an ideal offensive combination, I found that all previously tried systems had their marked disadvantages which tended to offset their strengths. This book specifically points out how the

Slot-I and its variations will provide an awesome attack that is diversified and flexible, as well as reliable and balanced to both sides of the line, inside and outside.

You can expect direct, yard-gaining benefits from the information contained in this book, as emphasized in the following list:

(1) The complexities of modern football will be broken down into a simple form that is easily understood and applied, and that is usable at all levels of play.

(2) Opponent defenses will be forced to play you balanced, allowing the Slot-I offense to make full use of its many alignment strengths and variations.

(3) Gambling overshifts by the defense, if attempted, will be subject to your complete arsenal at the undershifted side.

(4) The make-up of your pass offense will be easy to apply, yet will be demanding on your opposition.

(5) Your power-running game will be at full advantage, without sacrifice to deception or loss of your wide game to either side of the line.

(6) The strengths and talents of your personnel can be realized fully, without dependence upon groomed athletes at every position. Thereby, strong points can be emphasized while your weak points can be hidden or compensated for.

The Complete Guide to Winning Slot-I Football presents an offensive combination that has parts gathered from all sections of the country, which include high school, college and pro offenses. It departs from any form of emphasis placed on winning by overpowering your opponent. Rather, the emphasis is placed on renewed methods of making the threat of a forward pass a living part of your field attack.

As the title infers, the Slot-I formation is given complete analysis. While offensive systems will come and go, no doubt the Slot-I and its related wrinkles will continue to gain popularity across the country, and will take its place in football history as one of the great run-pass innovations of modern time.

KEN LYONS

CONTENTS

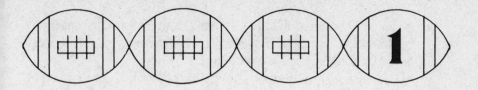

THE EVOLUTION OF
THE SLOT-I OFFENSE

Trends of offensive football invariably appear in cycles. Many innovations and tactics in vogue today are not "new" at all, but instead are a reintroduction of something discovered and used frequently in past generations of football. Since football's playing rules have undergone but few drastic changes since 1910, when the game had to be saved from its own self-destructiveness, the offensive makeup of the sport remains the same: strong blocking, hard running, quick execution, play timing, passing, catching, mental readiness and sound strategy.

The era of modern football began with the popularity of the center-quarterback ball exchange, which sent the bygone direct-snap formations into eventual exile. But, an understanding of proven systems of the past and present is necessary for us to gain in-depth knowledge of offensive football. Since the Slot-I is an end product of many diffused offensive cycles, a working knowledge of all proven offensive theories will help you use this information to develop your own personalized offense.

Probably one reason for the recurring cycles in offensive football is that the problems in coaching change very little. Whenever defensive tactics start catching up with offensive trends, a different approach must be sought, and so the familiar pattern of borrowing and swapping ideas begins once again. For example, you may have personnel problems, or perhaps your team's ability to move the football upfield has gradually become sluggish; consequently, answers must be sought in whatever source is available. The usual decisions that you must make are whether to concentrate more on power or on quickness, to use a tight or spread formation, to blend combinations of the latter, or to possibly try to improve upon deception and option-type plays.

The Tight-T offense of the 1940s established itself as the beginning of modern offensive football. When the concluding battles of the basic "T" and the direct-snap systems came to a head during the 1950s, the big evolution in offensive football began to unfold. From that time, football got a face-lift and would never again be as it was during its struggling years of development.

The decade of the 1950s became an era of the Split-T and the Wing-T. The Split-T broke all ties with theories of the Tight-T, while the Wing-T systems blended play-styles that were part "T" and part Single-Wing.

It was during the 1960s, however, that the big offensive boom took place. The rule-makers experiment with one-platoon football had ended, and offensive thinking began to transform from ball-control and field-position theories to wide-open philosophies of play. During the 60s, the quick-hitting Split-T began to wane and new fireworks began: the Flip-Flop T (a glamorized version of a Wing-T), the Multiple Pro-T, the Shifty-I (emphasizing Pro-I and Power-I sets) the Veer-T and the Wishbone-T. The Slot-I emerged with less fanfare in the mid 60s, and has since evolved into the sophisticated offense of today.

Many of the football refinements that were carried into the 1970s had their roots in the first rugby-type game between Princeton and Rutgers in 1869. Ironically, the T-formation itself can be traced back to the 1880s. Many coaching and playing techniques that we use today were developed into sound form in the early 1900s. Without the vision and groundwork laid by football's early pioneers, we would not have the scientific play that we enjoy today. A few of the notable predecessors of the modern football era are:

(1) The Single Wing System—innovated by Glenn "Pop" Warner of the Carlisle Indian School in 1910.

(2) The Notre Dame Box System—suggested by Amos Alonzo Stagg of the University of Chicago to Jesse Harper of Notre Dame. First used in 1913.

(3) The Double Wing System with an unbalanced line— innovated by "Pop" Warner in 1928.

(4) The TCU Spread System with a balanced line—innovated by Dutch Meyers of Texas Christian University.

(5) The SMU Spread System with an unbalanced line—innovated by Mattie Bell of Southern Methodist University.

(6) The Short Punt System—origin indefinite. Earliest account as a "massed formation" dates back to the game's earliest days. Updated and popularized at the University of Michigan in the 1920s by H.O. "Fritz" Crisler.

Now we shall dissect the modern era's offensive systems and analyze their strengths and weaknesses. All these systems have had their time and glory. Those systems that have lost their appeal fell victim, in most cases, to the defensive cycles that have caught up with them and made their offensive disadvantages outweigh their advantages.

THE TIGHT-T FORMATION

Apparent Running Strength:

Use of a quarterback under the center, in combination with three straight-hitting running backs, spaced evenly behind a balanced line, gives the "T" alignment (Diagram 1-1) unquestionable quickness and deception improvement over direct-snap formations. The Tight-T offensive system, as revitalized in the 1940s, makes varied use of double-team and trap blocking, along with motion-backs and flanker sets, in placing a variety of pressures on defensive alignments. Deception is personified by the quarterback as he carries out all ball-exchanges and faking with his back turned from the line of scrimmage, hiding the football from the defense with his body. Some of the favorite play-series of a Tight-T offense include straight hand-offs to each running back, off-tackle slants, inside and outside belly-plays, crossbucks, quick-pitches, middle-wedge plays, quarterback bootlegs and various trap plays.

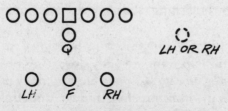

Diagram 1-1

Apparent Passing Strength:

A regular "T" can make effective use of play-action and bootleg pass combinations from each of its play series. Due to the quarterback's reverse-pivot ball handling, deception is to his advantage in hiding the football when disguising play-action passes. Sprint-out passes are effective from a Tight-T, but the use of motion-backs and flankers tends to broaden the possibility of an open-field passing offense, especially when throwing from a set pocket.

Apparent Running Weakness:

Over-conservative line splits invite modern "reading" defenses into pinching-off internal traps and off-tackle slants, resulting in piled-up bodies at the line of scrimmage. With a reluctance of reading defenses to allow themselves to be sucked inward on fake-and-pitch plays, the Tight-T can experience problems of choking-off its own running game if heavy reliance is placed on its full-house formation. When a motion-back or flanker is deployed to open up the attack, part of the inside running game becomes weakened or eliminated.

Apparent Passing Weakness:

Utilization of deep pass patterns by more than two receivers is difficult but not impossible to execute without a motion-back or set flanker. From the full "T" only the two ends are in a position to achieve quick, deep penetration into the defensive secondary.

Problem Areas:

Quarterback faking is heavily emphasized and necessary in a Tight-T attack. He should be mechanically adept in faking and a sure threat with the vital bootleg running and passing series. Pitch-out plays from a "T" alignment are difficult to perfect in timing, and this style of attack can not survive ill-timed ball handling. The success of wide plays is essential to establishing the internal ground game. Numerous blocking skills and techniques are required of *all* linemen!

NOTE: The full "T" alignment is acclaimed as one of the original formations from the early days of organized football. During the '40s, the Tight-T gave birth to many principles that are being put into practice today, although expanded through other offensive systems and concepts. From this

offense the coined phrase "running for daylight" had its early echoes, as a result of the opportunity found by running backs in picking holes following a deep hand-off.

Formation Revisionists: Clark Shaughnessy (Stanford) and George Halas (Chicago Bears) 1939-40. The earliest account of a "T" alignment dates back to 1888.

THE MULTIPLE-SHIFT OFFENSE

Apparent Strengths:

The best of direct-snap and "T" offensive attacks can be put into use as isolated play segments by making quick shifts into varying formations (Diagram 1-2). With the backfield moving around into changing positions, both the running and passing strength of the offense is changing constantly. Front-line defenders must worry about being outmanned internally and out-flanked at the corners. Pass receivers could find themselves wide open if a faulty adjustment is made to their varying positions. Some of the popular formations of a Multiple-Shift attack may include the Unbalanced-T, the Single Wing, the Notre Dame Box, the Minnesota "Y" formation, and variations of the Single and Double Wing-T. A center snap-back through the quarterback's legs to one of the running backs is also a popular innovation.

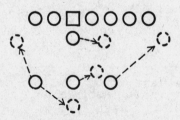

Diagram 1-2

Apparent Weaknesses:

The biggest pitfall a Multiple-Shift offense has to face is to avoid becoming its own victim rather than that of its opposition. As often is the case, a multiple-offensive team can attempt too many innovations, and thus lack the crispness, aggressiveness and play execution needed to be at its full potential. Secondly, multiple-offense systems may find its players unfamiliar with defensive adjustments made just before the ball snap. Therefore, quick and accurate recognition of a defensive alignment is *not* made, which can then result in poor play execution. A brainy quarterback is vital to calling change-of-play automatics at the line of scrimmage, along with a line intelligent enough to comprehend the changes in assignment. Lastly, opponents who have done their scouting and research "homework" can make an educated prediction about play trends and formation tendencies when facing a piecemeal offense.

Comment: The practice of mixing plays from unrelated offensive systems can result in inconsistency and a lack of continuity. A "bread and butter" play series that can be used from formation variations is important to team efficiency. Series of plays that are separate from each formation alignment can be as difficult to blend as oil and water. Too, a coach must be careful in combining factions that require a change in fundamental technique, such as ever-changing center-snap situations. When a Multiple-Shift attack has been successful, great care has been taken to perfect exact timing between the center and his corresponding backfield, with every variable having been taken into account.

Top Innovator: Biggie Munn (Michigan State University), 1947.

THE SPLIT-T FORMATION

Apparent Running Strength:

Large hole spacings in the line tend to isolate defenders at the point of attack, making them vulnerable to quick hand-off plays. If the defense refuses to split out with the offensive linemen, blocking angles will result. The strength of the Split-T (Diagram 1-3) lies in its ability to strike quickly over a broad plane. In its pure form, the Split-T offense did not intermix Tight-T concepts—all blocking is one-on-one and the basic plays are limited, usually to five at each side. These plays include a halfback dive, a fullback off-tackle, a quarterback option, a fullback counter and a quarterback counter. The hallmark of this offense is the action of the quarterback sliding down the line with precision ball handling. The Split-T thrives on finesse and deception rather than power. The heart of the offense is the halfback dive play, with its hand-off exchange taking place slightly inside the play hole.

Diagram 1-3

Apparent Passing Strength:

With the exception of a sprint-out pass, most Split-T pass plays begin off the fake of a running play. The quarterback can throw off a fake of the halfback' dive, the fullback off-tackle or the fullback counter. A running pass by either halfback is applicable from an option pitch. In theory, the passing game should merely supplement its possession-running attack for the purpose of keeping the secondary defense honest and capitalizing on defensive overcommitments.

Apparent Running Weakness:

If the option play is contained successfully, the Split-T attack loses much of its effectiveness. One-on-one blocking techniques must be mastered by the linemen—the offense in its basic form does not use double-team, cross, trap or sweep blocking. If the battle is lost to the defense at the neutral zone, this type of offense will go nowhere!

Apparent Passing Weakness:

The Split-T passing attack is generally limited. The deep passing threat is lean, with only two receivers—the ends—on the proximity of the line. A two-deep secondary with agile cornerbacks can do a respectable job of coping with most Split-T pass patterns.

Problem Areas:

As with all "pure" offensive systems, time breeds familiarity. Whatever proves simple for the offense eventually becomes simple for the defense to recognize. The Split-T is still a sound offense, but it has lost much of its appeal because ball-control (possession) tactics have given way to more open methods of attack. Over-popularity proved to be its worst enemy, and the "have nots" began searching for greater diversity.

> **Note: Although traps, off-tackle slants, and inside and outside belly plays are not a part of the basic series, many coaches include these plays in their team offense. Also, many perennial collegiate powers that used a Split-T found it necessary to loosen concentrated defenses with a wide flanker. When a flanker set was used, various trap plays were installed, usually to fill the void left by a vacated halfback or fullback.**

Formation & Play-Series Innovator: Don Faurot (Missouri), 1941. Chief Disciples: James Tatum (Maryland & North Carolina) and Bud Wilkinson (Oklahoma).

THE WING-T FORMATION

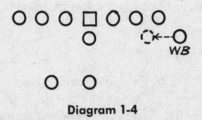

Diagram 1-4

Apparent Running Strength:

Early versions of the Wing-T included both balanced and unbalanced lines, and made considerable use of lateral-movement plays similar to Single-Wing attacks. Later Wing-T systems evolved into hybrid concepts, with the halfback side primarily Split-T and the wingback side a combination of Tight-T and Single Wing (Diagram 1-4). A flip-flop of all Wing-T personnel, a steal from the Single Wing's "turnover principle," was popularized by the University of Texas in 1961, which reemphasized the value of specialization and simplicity of play assignments. An outstanding feature of the Wing-T alignment is a strong, power-sweep play threat at the wing side. Aside from the Split-T series, deception is also favorable with inside and outside reverses, various fullback and halfback traps and a comprehensive belly-play series. In general analysis, the Wing-T formation can strike both quickly and powerfully, with an above-par passing advantage.

Apparent Passing Advantage:

A sprint-out pass can be used effectively from both the wingback and halfback sides. Play-action passes are a positive factor from a Wing-T alignment. Drop-back passes can also be used without significant problems, although they are more practical with split receivers. The wingback side gives a better deep-pass advantage over the halfback side.

Apparent Running Weakness:

A closed formation such as the Wing-T is usually dependent upon finesse to the "T" side, and a power game to the open side, although slants, isolations, traps and belly plays can be inter-mingled. However, since the defense does not have to thin itself out in covering the basic formation, a defensive match of manpower can hurt a Wing-T offense. In short, a physical offense is reliant upon physical personnel.

Apparent Passing Weakness:

Although the offense does have three quick receivers at its disposal, the defensive secondary is not forced to spread and cover the open field. If a split end is used opposite the wingback side, the passing attack can be opened up, but only at the expense of a weakened running game off-tackle to that side.

Problem Areas:

Since the power sweep is a key play in the Wing-T offense, its effectiveness must be established to give virility to the remaining attack. Since this play is slow in turning the corner, a well-controlled double-team block is vital at the point of attack. Physical linemen at the wing side and a skilled blocker at fullback are important, along with a speedy halfback to turn up into the northbound traffic before defensive congestion builds up.

Note: The Slot-T has many of the same ingredients as a Wing-T attack. The major difference is the location of the wingback

between the tackle and the end, instead of outside the end. A tight spacing within the slot does give a Slot-T certain advantages over the regular Wing-T, as far as blocking patterns and hidden misdirection plays are concerned.

Early Prototype: Amos Alonzo Stagg (Springfield College) designed a Diamond-T in 1890, which consisted of a full-house backfield with both ends set back as wingbacks. In 1910, a ruling was passed requiring a minimum of seven linemen on the line of scrimmage.

Winged-T Innovator: Frank Kavanaugh (Dartmouth), 1919. Popularized by Lou Little (Columbia), Dave Nelson (Delaware) and Forrest Evashevski (Iowa).

THE MULTIPLE PRO-T

Apparent Running Strength:

The movement of the tailback (or fullback) into various positions—both tight end and split end sides—can pose many problems of varying strength concentrations to the opposing defense. In a Multiple Pro-T concept (Diagram 1-5), the tailback is not limited to one side only. It is commonplace to move the running backs around in a broken-halfback set, an overload power set (all backs aligned on one side), and a split-back set. This tactic gives varying degrees of running advantages and pass receiver vantage points.

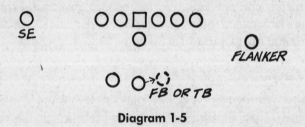

Diagram 1-5

Apparent Passing Strength:

Split receivers in any system will give maximum passing opportunity, providing the quarterback talent is sufficient to take advantage of the resources. Three receivers are located to release quickly and burden the defensive secondary with deep pass routes, while the running backs can share time as a fourth receiver on designated pass patterns. The varying positions of the running backs can give a balanced pass release threat one time, and a flood receiver advantage the next time. A tackle-eligible pass play can be used in leagues where the rules permit.

Apparent Running Weaknesses:

Unfortunately, teams that use multiple alignments usually give play tendencies that can be charted easily. Such teams usually have a few pet plays that are run from each formation selection (though it may be a subconscious tendency), or certain pet plays that are run to one side only.

Apparent Passing Weaknesses:

With a competent quarterback there are few technical passing weaknesses in Pro-T alignments. A common problem is locating an athlete on the squad who is a capable blocker at the tight-end position, who is also capable of being an outstanding pass receiver (speed and cutting ability are helpful here). Because of the location of the tight end in the passing game, the offense could find itself with the problem of having its two best receivers spaced apart with a poor receiver separating them. (Two talented receivers working together on patterns place the greatest demands on secondary coverages.) Another problem involves the backfield shift into an overload power set: the weak side passing game may be restricted to one receiver unless there is pressure from the strong side receivers crossing over.

Problem Areas:

Busted plays, backfield confusion (with assignment indecision) and play-call tendencies will be a problem with this system if the team is not carefully drilled. A gifted quarterback, who can think under pressure and make intelligent automatics at the line of scrimmage, is a necessity in running a Multiple Pro-T. In recent seasons, defensive teams have employed tactics using a three-deep secondary with a "five-under" zone coverage and a three man rush; this has tended to choke off drop-back passing attacks.

Comment: When the tailback is shifted to the tight side, all the direct running-game force is concentrated to that side,

with a simulation to the might and resulting weaknesses of the single wing.

Innovators: The professional coaches, especially during the era of the "Three-End T" of the late 1950s.

THE SHIFTY-I FORMATIONS

Apparent Running Strength:

The instantaneous movement from a four running-back power formation into a spread receiver set (Diagram 1-6) is enough to worry any defense. Basic football plays can be run from these quick shifts. A talented running back can be placed in many positions, both as a runner and receiver. From the I-back position, a talented tailback can hit all the holes along the line of scrimmage equally, to both the right and the left. In theory the idea is to run a few basic plays from varying formations.

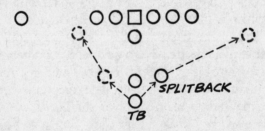

Diagram 1-6

Apparent Passing Strength:

The varying placement of shifting receivers keeps pressure on the secondary in making proper formation recognition and adjustment. The receiver strength of the formation may be balanced at one time and unbalanced the next. Some football teams "walk" an up-back into the tight-end position at either side as the wide receivers make the adjustments into split end or flanker back positions.

Popular Formations:

The Power-I, the Pro-I (wide flanker with an opposite split end), the Walking-I (a version of the original Nugent Full-I), the Pro-T alignments, and the Slot-I.

Apparent Running Weakness:

The Shifty-I offense has the same weaknesses as the Multiple Pro-T offense—play tendencies and pet plays are often run from a pet formation to a pet side.

Apparent Passing Weaknesses:

The Shifty-I has almost the identical problems of the Multiple Pro-T systems: throwing efficiency is mandatory; the tight end must perform as a blocker and an effective receiver; a good weak-side pass attack is sometimes lacking from overload power sets. When the offense aligns in a Power-I set, the passing disadvantages are similar to the Split-T attack. (If the tight end gets held up on his attempted release from the line of scrimmage, the offense becomes trimmed down to one quick receiver who can go deep.)

Problem Areas:

It is easy to get carried away with the frills and forget the basics. If simplicity and soundness are not a part of the teaching process, a team may find it is beating itself during game-night competition.

Comment: The full-house Power-I formation is similar to the strengths of the Notre Dame Box system. The I-formation offense, like the "T" offense, was slow to gain acceptance, but finally had such an impact on football that it changed offensive football at all levels, including the professional.

Formation Innovators: Tom Nugent (Virginia Military Institute) 1949. Popularized and expanded into its modern trends by John McKay (Southern California) in the early 1960s. The first recorded backfield shift to change a formation's strength was initiated by Amos Alonzo Stagg (University of Chicago) in 1904.

THE VEER-T

Apparent Running Strength:

A balanced running threat based on the triple (veer) option (Diagram 1-7) can be used to both sides, regardless of flanker-back positions. The basic veer-play series is usually featured—the triple-option, the halfback counter, the counter-option, and the outside-veer option (off tackle). The triple-option play is an offense in itself, threatening at the inside crease (over guard), at the middle crease (QB keep over tackle), and the outside crease (pitch). The outside-veer play tends to disrupt the defensive keys against the triple-option because the three options are moved over one hole to the outside, placing the dive back off-tackle. Most Veer-T teams also include the standard, two-way option with the quarterback taking a drop-step, sprinting at the defensive end and optioning his reaction (the on-side set back serves as a lead blocker). Other advantages include simplicity in blocking rules and the dive back's relationship with the defensive tackle—a "false key" is not as easily given at the inside seam because the runner hits the hole more directly than he would from a centralized position behind the quarterback.

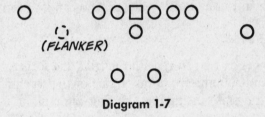

Diagram 1-7

Apparent Passing Strength:

Play-action passes with complementary drop-back passes go well with the Veer-T. Three receivers are continually releasing upfield, which keeps the defensive secondary in limbo as to whether the offense is going to run or pass. With two, or possibly three receivers in a spread position, there is ample opportunity to exploit secondary breakdowns. Also, the set backs are in a good position to slip out into the short flat or flare as an outlet receiver, when the outside pressure is hampering the drop-back passing attack.

Apparent Running Weakness:

Finesse is required of the quarterback—he must be an aggressive runner and an adequate passer or the offense will go nowhere. Both set backs must be physically tough inside and quick in getting to the corner for the pitch. The tight end serves as a lead blocker at the corner when the triple-option is run to his side, but he does not have as good blocking leverage as does a blocking halfback from the

Wishbone-T. A fumbled pitch away from the tight-end side has less security against a defensive recovery on a loose ball.

Apparent Passing Weakness:

The Veer-T is a strong passing formation in structure, provided that the quarterback can handle both the run and the pass, and that the tight end is a strong pass receiver. If you are not willing to put the ball in the air, you would be better off running a triple-option series from a tighter formation.

Problem Areas:

If the triple (veer) option is not perfected, a change in play format is in order with this formation. Intelligent pass calls are necessary in order to take advantage of the pursuit miscues and any rotations attempted by the defensive secondary. If the defense can not be kept completely honest, problems will occur. If the play mechanics are not perfected and placed in the hands of a cool-headed quarterback, the offense may become the "fumbling veer."

> **Comment: The Veer-T rekindled a nearly forgotten football axiom: football games are won by simplicity, poise and execution. The final ingredient is player material; if it can be found to fit the needs of the Veer-T, the opposing defenses will have their hands full. Like the original Split-T, the Veer-T wins by perfect play execution.**

Inside Veer-Option Innovator: Homer Rice (Highland High School, Ft. Thomas, Ky.) 1957, from a "Short-T" alignment. Popularized by Bill Yeoman (University of Houston).

THE WISHBONE-T

Apparent Running Advantages:

The Wishbone formation (Diagram 1-8) gives the power aspect to the triple-option (veer) play. The triple-option play forces three distinct option points at the line of scrimmage, with the benefit of a lead blocker on the final (pitch) phase. The close alignment of the fullback gives the offense a quick thrust at the inside crease, over guard. The quarterback exploits the middle crease—off tackle— with added pressure placed at the middle crease by an application of "load" blocking, which calls for the lead blocking-back to block the defensive end. The inside-belly play, off-tackle, also puts a strain on defensive attempts to contain the triple-option play. The counter play to the halfback and the counter-option play serve to keep a check on reckless pursuit. Wishbone-T enthusiasts claim that the mesh point between the quarterback and the fullback is superior to the dive-back relationship of a Veer-T formation.

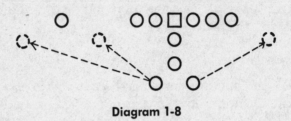

Diagram 1-8

Apparent Passing Advantages

The play-action pass is best utilized off of this type of attack. Fakes can be used from the fullback-ride phase, from the fake-of-the-counter play or from the fake-of-the-counter option. Passes to the split end can especially be exploited; both ends, however, have the advantage of splitting zone-secondary creases, as the opponent becomes preoccupied with stopping the triple-option. With the ends releasing into the secondary on every option play, the defense has continuous force applied to it. The split end does have an open field advantage in running "out" patterns, inside "curls" and deep "post" routes. Breaking the backfield into slot, wing and flanker back formations can give more imaginative pass-route combinations.

Apparent Running Weaknesses:

If heavy reliance is placed on reading the defense on the option, it is usually necessary to make game-time adjustments on the manipulation of the triple-option play. From each opponent, special defensive maneuvers, stunts, assignment switching, and special alignments likely will be seen. Veer-T promoters claim that the fullback, from his standard position, is easier for a defensive tackle to "false key" on the triple-option, while the Veer-T halfback hits quicker and the quarterback's hand-off is more decisive. This controversy has pros and cons on both sides, but it is vital that any triple-option quarterback be an aggressive runner or else the defense will concede his option point and concentrate on the other two options. Without the threat of a triple-option play, the Wishbone offense should use its lead blocking back on base-option plays, cross-bucks, inside-belly plays and sweeps, which can be supplemented with a tight wingback or slot back.

Apparent Passing Weakness:

With only two quick-releasing receivers from the full-house set, this offense is not classified as a deep-passing offense. If the receivers cannot find a breakdown in the secondary coverage, the passing game may suffer in trying to save problem games. A passing threat must be established, or else the offense may begin facing rotating nine-man fronts. It is futile for a ball-control offense to play catch-up, when its passing attack cannot make big plays.

Problem Areas:

An option play of some kind is a necessity in a Wishbone offense. Quarterback talent and a rugged fullback are essential. The halfbacks must love blocking. If the triple-option is used in its pure reading form (leaving two unblocked defenders on the line of scrimmage), *all* available time must be spent on it. Because of the intricate play mechanics of the triple-option, there can be little time left for other play categories.

Formation Innovators: Charles Cason (Monnig Jr. High of Ft. Worth) 1952. Triple Option version devised by Emory Bellard and Darrell Royal (University of Texas) 1968.

THE SLOT-I OFFENSE

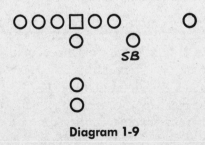

Diagram 1-9

In subsequent chapters, the advantages of the Slot-I offense (Diagram 1-9) shall be broadened and discussed. The specific advantages of the Slot-I follow. In this analysis, the advantages of other established offensive systems can be put together into a single package within a Slot-I attack.

Specific Advantages:

1. The Slot-I formation is potentially strong at the off-tackle lanes, both to the tight and the slot sides. Off-tackle power slants are effective in short yardage and goal-line situations. The Slot-I is a great "challenge" offense when faced with tough yardage.

2. Flip-flopping of personnel allows for simplicity, specialization of abilities and exploitation of defensive weaknesses at the line of scrimmage and in the defensive secondary.

3. A four-back running game gives maximum running power and deception plus a passing threat of three quick-releasing receivers which places tremendous stress on all defensive coverages. Since the slot back has a dual role as a running back and receiver, this system is superior to the wide flanker-back formations: "The whole is greater than the sum of its parts."

4. Centralized running backs allow a mirrored attack, freeing the best runner at the tailback position to strike equally at all points along the line of scrimmage. Therefore, daylight-running opportunity is gained and compensations can be made for any blocking miscues or defensive over-pursuit. A talented runner can be put to the best use when given more opportunities to run with the football and the capability of hitting with equal balance anywhere along the line of scrimmage.

5. Quickness, power and deception can be utilized over a broad front. The tandem alignment of the running backs gives the fullback the advantage of quick strikes from tackle to tackle. The fullback is in the ideal position to set up fake-and-give deception and to fill the role of the key backfield blocker; the tailback's alignment gives the ideal position from which to utilize clever footwork on power plays, fake-and-gives and pitch-outs; and the slot back is

aligned in a position to run misdirection plays both inside and wide.

6. Defensive slants, blitzes and secondary rotations can be controlled. Opposing defenses cannot load up on both the running and passing sides at the same time.

7. Third and long yardage situations can best be overcome from a slot attack, since the two best receivers are aligned to the same side and can be used to exploit the deep flat.

8. Passes from off-tackle play-action, quick-opener, bootleg and pull-up techniques can be utilized within a simplified plan of attack. Pass-coverage "holes" within the defensive secondary can be expanded easily, and man-to-man coverage is often forced unwillingly upon the opponent.

9. The pull-up passing technique can aid a shorter quarterback's field vision and pass delivery, since less mechanical skill is required. Also, the semi-sprint action of a pull-up pass helps the quarterback get away from the full defensive line charge and linebacker blitzes, without giving up his freedom to attack the entire defensive perimeter. The use of the tandem backs as lead blockers on pull-up passes can be an invaluable aid in coping with eight-man front defenses. If the quarterback is an effective runner, sprint-out passes can pose still another threat to the defensive perimeter.

10. The Slot-I is simple in its structure, complete in its representation of all major play categories, flexible in adjustments, and capable of adapting to all defensive alignments week after week.

Apparent Shortcomings:

At first glance, it may appear that the Slot-I has a certain difficulty attacking the corner flat at the tight-end side with advantageous pass patterns. Taking note of this, a remedy has been found which will be explained in the next paragraph. But perhaps the biggest shortcoming of a Slot-I alignment can be pointed out by Slot-T proponents. First, from a Slot-T formation, the fullback plays a more versatile role in carrying the football with sweeps, counters and a quicker striking off-tackle power play. Second, from a Slot-T formation, the tailback is in a position to run a straight-ahead dive play and can turn the corner quicker on a quick-pitch play. These opposing views have their merit and, in fact, supplemental "T" alignments can be included easily for reasons of versatility, providing the plays remain similar and are kept simple. The counterpoints in defense of the Slot-I will follow.

Compensations and Counterpoints:

The first compensation that must be made to remedy the single-receiver alignment at the tight side is to make use of the fullback "Waggle" pass into the flat to that side. Other bootleg-pass plays may be included as well. Secondly, by sliding a running back out of the backfield on play-action passes, the defense must keep its pass coverage honest to that side, or get burned by an uncovered receiver.

In response to Slot-T comparisons, the Slot-I's tailback is more fluid in running the off-tackle power play, which allows a better cutting advantage, in addition to the fact that off-tackle plays can be run by the best runner available to both sides of the line with equal latitude. It is true that the Slot-I tailback is not in a dive-back position, but he certainly does not have a handicap in hitting the interior defense quickly from the Isolate play alone. The fullback, however, must assume the role of a dive-back to have a complete attack in any I-formation system. In reference to the quick-pitch play, both the quick-pitch and sweep are one and the same to an I-back, depending upon the up-front blocking pattern. If onside linemen are pulled to lead the pitch play, speed is essential, from an "I" backfield, to outrun an unblocked defender. But, an I-back sweep, with only the backside guard pulling from the line, is more secure and will actually reach the corner sooner than a "T" sweep from a halfback position.

Some critics of the Slot-I alignment may point out that the duties of each running back are limited—but this "shortcoming" is, in actuality, one of its strengths. This offensive concept is one of specialization! It allows for *adaptability* in placing athletic talent and disguising personnel weaknesses. On the contrary, it is a relatively easy task to add more plays to the basic offensive attack, and have all running backs attempt to strike at the defense in more ways, *if* this were desirable and necessary.

Problem Areas:

A clever and/or rugged runner at the tailback position is a *vital* necessity in any I-formation attack. He should have the tenacity to fight through hand-tackling efforts and the balance to stay on his feet! It is imperative that the tailback be drilled in making tough yardage in challenging situations! If a solid runner at tailback does not materialize, supplemental running-back variations should be included within the framework of the Slot-I.

Opinion: The Slot-I offense is an exceptionally *comprehensive* attack within itself, but can be branched out easily with formation variations to adapt to a team's personnel needs. It is a complete and flexible offense that offers the *best in football* when properly organized and patiently taught.

WRAP UP

In this chapter, I have made an attempt to generalize the time-tested offensive styles of play. All fundamentally sound offensive systems will win ball games for you when team members take pride in blocking techniques, when passing and catching skills are developed and when squad morale is favorable. The Slot-I system can not make any exception to this. It can only unify the best of other styles into a simplified and complete offense, giving you more time to teach perfect execution.

The Slot-I evolved from the Shifty-I offensive system. As it was adopted by various universities, its popularity spread at all levels of play as a separate offense of its own. Its most appealing attraction was the demonstrated ease with which a power offense could be used, without expense to an equally strong passing game. Statistically, the universities that used the Slot-I have illustrated a positive balance in running and passing yardage.

You will find that the outstanding strength of the Slot-I formation is in its structural ability to run and pass effectively on a 50/50 percent basis, with considerable allowances made for placement of average personnel. The Slot-I's offensive balance comes from the formation's superior structure and adaptability, the accessability of its four running backs and its compatability with a great number of play series.

The following chapters discuss the functional development of a Slot-I offensive attack. The next two chapters cover objectives and procedures—the planning and methods areas—that are the building stones of this version of a Slot-I offense. Fundamentals, assignments and the formulation of a flexible "keystone offense" complete the book, enabling you to gain a better understanding of the **WHYS** and **HOWS** of the Slot-I formation and its variations.

Credit: The Slot-I was popularized as a separate offense by Frank Broyles (University of Arkansas) 1964.

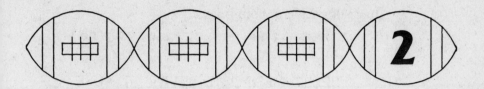

PLANNING OBJECTIVES FOR THE SLOT-I OFFENSE

Efficiency in offensive football demands purpose. Without purpose your team offense will never achieve the full potential of its player or alignment strength. It is vital, therefore, that you know exactly what you expect to accomplish with an offense before any realistic results can be expected. *Prior to each and every football game, the offensive coach and quarterbacks should review the objectives intended for their offense!* Without objectives, a team cannot expect to gain an advantage over an opponent of equal caliber since purpose and exploitation is the motivating force of offensive football.

Four general objectives are suggested to serve as guideposts to offensive thinking, planning and strategy. The potential of an offense lies primarily in the mind of the coach in charge of the offense, in that personal ability to define his offensive purpose and then to apply this philosphy during game competition. Offensive initiative guided by a crystal clear plan can make the difference between a run-of-the-mill attack and an explosive one.

The four objectives that guide our Slot-I offensive system are listed below and shall be followed by detailed explanations of each.

1. Attack with balance from your offense.

2. Keep the defense in a bind with a specialized power running side and a specialized passing side.

3. Attack off-tackle to both sides.

4. Use the forward pass as a basic offensive weapon.

HOW TO PUT THESE OBJECTIVES INTO USE

I. Attack with balance from your offense.

    A. Strive to implement the ideal combination of running and passing while maintaining consistency. With the Slot-I formation, you have a more comprehensive two-way threat of the run-and-pass. An ideal blend of both of the once-divided schools of thought should be sought, since the formation is compatible to both styles of play.

    B. Establish an effective *first-down* attack from tackle to tackle so that the slot concept of the offense can double the run-pass pressure on the defense. You should make this two-way threat continuous, and it will be effective on the goal line as well. Make the defense have second thoughts about bunching up on the Slot-I formation at *any* time, for fear of a sudden-death pass.

    C. Make thorough use of the fake-and-give plays that this unique offense has proven sound and reliable. Sequence plays are invaluable in giving the Slot-I attack deception, which is lacking in many of the present I-formation systems.

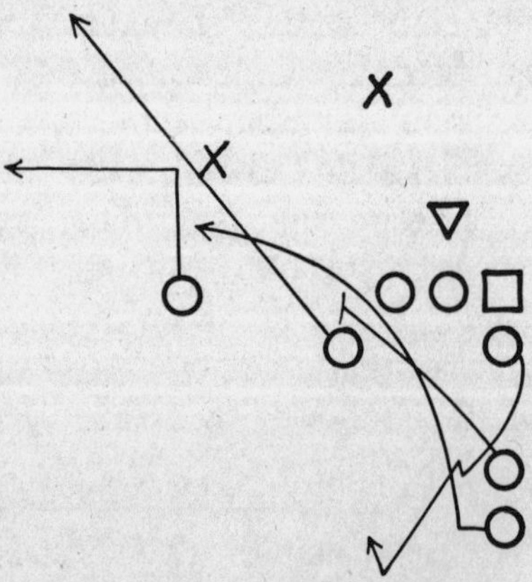

Diagram 2-1 Spread Concept

D. Call upon the separate passing, quick-hitting and power combinations of the offense. The integrated concept of the Slot-I combines three proven elements of previous systems:

   (1) A *Spread-side* passing and running attack (See Diagram 2-1). The Slot Side excels in passing without weakening the running game or losing formation balance. Some of the traditions borrowed from other spread-formation systems include pull-up and sprint-out passes, draw and screen plays, and inside shield blocking by split receivers on wide plays.

   (2) A *T-formation* type of attack (See Diagram 2-2). Unilateral quickness and deception are emphasized and explored. Some of the traditions that are borrowed from the "T" include adjustable line spacings, dive plays, counters, fake-and-gives, and bootleg runs and passes. Also not to be overlooked are the concepts of mirrored plays to both sides of the line, front-out hand-offs (Split-T) and reverse-out hand-offs with the innovative use of motion and fly-backs (Tight-T).

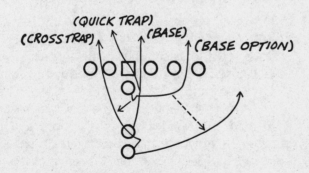

Diagram 2-2 A "T" Concept

   (3) A *Single-Wing* application of power-blocking methods (See Diagram 2-3). Pulling linemen, trapping, double-teaming, lead-back blocks and flip-flop linemen all are components borrowed from yes-

teryear. When applied at the Slot-I's tight side, the Single-Wing type plays may go opposite corner rotations made by the defensive secondary. Reverses and bootlegs are part of the grand scheme.

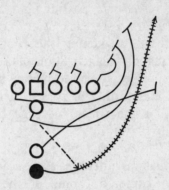

Diagram 2-3 A Single-Wing Concept (tailback sweep)

Opinion: While many modern offensive systems lay claim to a merger of Spread, "T" and Single-Wing strengths, the Slot-I's centralization of running balance and built-in passing versatility can blend all of these attack features within a single formation structure. This resourcefulness leads to simplicity in teaching and player understanding and execution.

E. Organize your weekly game plan to assure that the play calls *complement* each other. Power slants, fullback leads, pitch-outs, options, quick-opener dives, traps, and misdirection plays are coupled with four easy-to-learn pass attack methods: The pull-up pass method and a play-action pass method, which becomes subdivided into bootleg run-pass options and pass play fakes off quick-opener (Base) and off-tackle (Power) plays. With the exception of bootleg passes, identical pass patterns are used with each of the pass attack methods. Many of our passes may be thrown from a sprint-out instead of a pull-up, but to us this is considered a luxury that is dependent upon a quarterback's running ability. Both our running play and pass play categories are meant to set each other up without ever resorting to calling plays at random, without purpose. For example, a fullback quick-opener up the middle can set up a dive-hole Cross Trap (See Diagram 2-4). Also, a linebacker Isolation play can be used to set up a quarterback option or keeper (See Diagram 2-5). And, pass plays that force a perimeter rotation toward the slot side can open up many possibilities to the opposite side (See Diagram 2-6). There are unlimited resources available from a Slot-I offense.

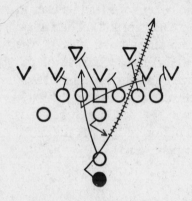

Diagram 2-4 Cross Trap

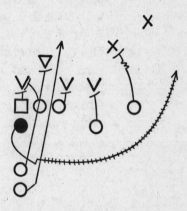

Diagram 2-5 Slot Side Keeper

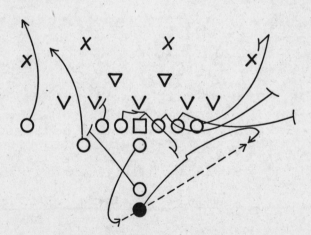

Diagram 2-6 Opposite Rotation

F. Make appropriate use of the tremendous option play advantages of the Slot-I formation. Several options can be used effectively, but care should be taken in your selection. Many option types are not as intimidating as others, but are safer and more reliable. Your selection should depend entirely upon personnel abilities and their level of experience—not upon your personal philosphy or chalkboard theory. The Base Option is simple to execute and has the advantage of an inside fake (See Diagram 2-7). The Lead Option is without a play fake but has the advantage of giving a pass-read key to the defense, plus the benefit of a lead blocker in front of the ball pitch (See Diagram 2-8). The Isolate Option is the slower developing option play of the three, but can cause a well-defined collapse of the defense, plus the advantage of a fourth running back (the slot back) as the pitch man (See Diagram 2-9). If other selections are considered, just remember that play execution and ball-handling security is the name of the game in any option-play series!

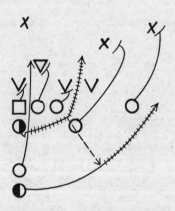

Diagram 2-7 Base Option

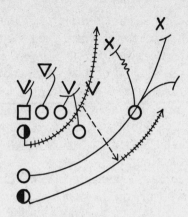

Diagram 2-8 Lead Option

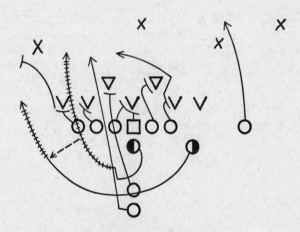

Diagram 2-9 Isolate Option

G. Take care in adding special plays to your offense. The Slot-I can be complete without a congestion of plays. Proper organization is the key. There should be few waste products—unnecessary plays that are not a functional part of a play series should be rejected.

H. Remember, sustained-drive tactics do have a place in football, especially when used as a change-of-pace measure. Consistency is the byword rather than "three yards and a cloud of dust." Ball-control measures are tactical means of:

(1) Running the clock.

(2) Protecting a lead.

(3) Settling your offensive unit down when emotionally high-strung.

(4) Keeping an opponent's potent offensive team members sitting on the bench.

(5) Going for a "sure score" via high-percentage running plays.

Note: Keep in mind that success on offense will be better assured *if* the opposition must fear *all avenues* of your offensive attack; therefore, a meticulous blend of all attack methods and strategies will improve your chances of success.

II. Keep the defense in a bind with a specialized power-running side and a specialized passing side.

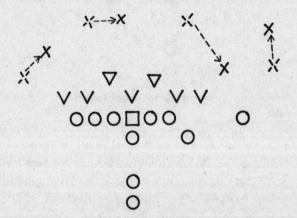

Diagram 2-10 Run or Pass Opposite Defensive Commitment

A. Force the defense to cover a run-oriented side and a pass-oriented side. Then you should attack opposite any defensive over-commitment that is made to either side. A general rule of thumb is to throw if the slot side is covered ineffectively, and to run if the passing threat is over-covered (See Diagram 2-10). Special secondary coverages, such as pre-rotations, perimeter rolls at a select corner, or double-coverage of receivers, will be at the opponent's disadvantage in defending the tight side of the Slot-I offense. If the defense is balanced, then use both the run and the pass.

B. Place your opponent in jeopardy when stunts, loops or line slants are attempted. A prime advantage of a Slot-I formation is that slanting tactics off a 5-2 Rover defense can be contained with trap, angle and double-team blocking. The off-tackle Trap, Power and inside Isolate plays are effective, and the Quick Trap up the middle has an excellent chance of breaking clean, both toward and away from the defensive slant call (See Diagram 2-11).

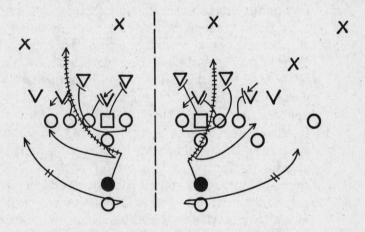

Diagram 2-11 Quick Trap vs. Slants

C. Force the defense to loosen its corners with the passing game before running wide. When passing and running plays are mixed properly, your offense can use variety and a change of play tempo to keep the defense loose. Then you have a better chance of controlling the offensive outcome of the game, and more first downs and touchdowns are within your reach (See Diagram 2-12).

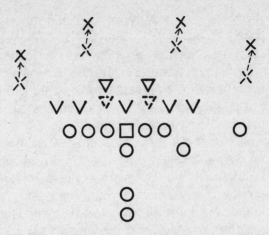

Diagram 2-12 Loosening the Corners

D. Pressure the defense with your overall game plan on the first two offensive downs, then use the remaining non-punting downs to maintain a chain of first downs. Field position should be foremost in consideration with all play selections, because you must determine when to rely on a forward pass or on play quickness, power or deception. Ordinarily, you will have to adapt your game-plan strategy to the defensive tactics used by the opponent.

E. Challenge the defense at the neutral zone in tough yardage situations if the opposition remains in its basic alignment. But, if a "ganged-up" defense is confronted, once again you should not hesitate to call a play-action or running pass. Develop team confidence in its "ground challenge and air security" training by instilling discipline and determination through repeated practice work within the goal-line area. Your team should be mentally and physically conditioned to whip the defense at the front line for vital footage, and to penetrate its air cover for open yardage when the opponent appears intimidated!

III. Attack off-tackle to both sides.

A. Use your slot back in a blocking role comparable to the tight end. A prime advantage of a Slot-I set is that it is an effective off-tackle formation *without* a loss of running versatility in its spread attack. Although the slot side of the line is pass-oriented, it does have an equal mechanical advantage in blocking for productive yardage (See Diagram 2-13).

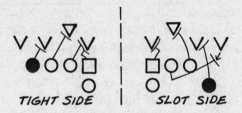

Diagram 2-13 Comparative Blocking Roles

B. Keep your poise when facing the inevitable third-and-long yardage situation. Make use of a secure sideline pass pattern, or pass underneath deep-covering defenders, using maximum blocking protection by your "I" backs from a pull-up pocket. But also consider a play-action pass to your tailback as he releases out of the backfield, in addition to a screen pass or draw play. Don't overlook the possibility of running at a conspicuous weakness shown in the opponent's "pass-prevent" coverage.

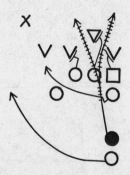

Diagram 2-14 The Starting Point of a Belly Series

C. Establish a sequence of belly-series plays to assure continuity in your offensive drives. The Slot-I is well adapted to belly-series faking, both to the fullback and the tailback. Mix up fullback and tailback hand-offs, alternating from the "fast ball" to a deliberate change-of-pace. In the Slot-I attack, a good combination is to have your fullback concentrate on most of the line-slicing plays and allow your tailback to run the across-the-grain and lateral plays (See Diagram 2-14).

D. Control short-yardage situations. Make the defense keep its commitment to covering the slot side passing game, so that your off-tackle plays remain open. In fact, the Double-Slot formation can force the defense to spread itself and give an advantage in using your fullback play-series inside the tackle lanes.

(1) Use high-percentage plays in goal line areas when your back is to it and when you are facing it.

(2) Never risk a cheap touchdown for the opponent by making a dangerous play selection in the critical field zone.

(3) Remember "what got you there" after a long drive into scoring territory, and *stay* with it.

E. Make selective use of full-house formations. A Power-I set, consisting of standard plays, can be easily included in your attack as a *supplementary* offense. Below are some common-sense reasons why the Power-I may be helpful:

(1) It gives added blocking mass at the strong side off-tackle hole (See Diagram 2-15).

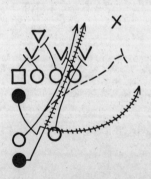

Diagram 2-15 Off-Tackle Blocking

(2) It can be a valuable supplement in exploring defensive areas just as the Double-Slot formation is valuable in exploring pass-attack areas.

(3) A Power-I attack, although limited, is good against teams that make few significant adjustments to a loaded formation.

(4) It is a means of giving *added muscle* to short-yardage sustained drives, especially if your offensive line is having difficulty in sustaining its blocking contact. An extra blocker from the backfield can be used to reinforce line blocking and help pick up floating linebackers. A concentration of force is evident, especially on the Isolate play that is aimed at an inside linebacker (See Diagram 2-16).

Diagram 2-16 Inside Concentration

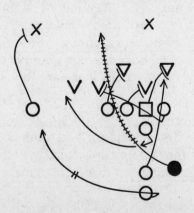

Diagram 2-17 Split-Side Finesse

(5) A balanced ground game can be accomplished by specializing part of the Slot I's finesse series to the split-end side, to complement the concentration of blocking force at the strong side (See Diagram 2-17).

(6) Part of the passing game can be retained by use of standard routes against single coverage (See Diagram 2-18).

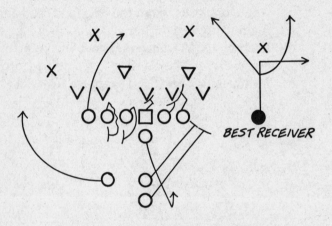

Diagram 2-18 Testing Single Coverage

Comment: With the Slot-I as the basic weapon, a Power-I supplement can serve best, when used on a stand-by basis, in much the same way as a "two-minute offense." It must be worked on, but too much time should not be spent on it. Its presence in the offensive repertoire, however, does give the offensive team a *broader base* in gaining additional flexibility to overcome any odds you may face in a given ball game.

IV. Use the forward pass as a basic offensive weapon.
    A. Have far-reaching goals in your philosphy of attack. Your thoughts must be directed toward touchdowns, not first downs. Learn how to make first downs work

for you in giving *more opportunity* to pick away at the lapses in the opponent's secondary defense.

B. Have a positive attitude toward winning with the passing attack. Do your part in planting the seeds of the "magic of believing!" The coach and the offensive line must believe in their quarterback and receivers, and the quarterback and receivers must have a deep respect for their offensive line and coach.

C. Be bold enough to go for a long-gainer in key situations. This is the only way you can have a true run-pass offensive attack. By grabbing the initiative, all avenues of strategy can be explored. Never limit your own potential.

D. Have a mental picture of what you intend to accomplish with your passing game. The coach and quarterback must know and understand how their pass plays are to be blended with the running plays. Maintain a mental picture, during the game, as to how the opponent is covering your offensive formation and as to the adjustments that have been made to an obvious passing situation.

E. Design creative "specials," and don't be afraid to make a one-receiver route adjustment during a game. Providing the alterations are consistent with your blocking assignments and can be easily executed, special innovations can break an otherwise tight game wide open. During your week of preparation for an upcoming game, special patterns should be considered so that you may capitalize upon certain give-away keys that are detected in your opponent's secondary. For example, a special cross-over pattern to the tight side can be installed, to exploit a secondary's commitment to contain off-tackle and keeper plays (See Diagram 2-19). Also, a defensive secondary "roll," which is common in reading veer-option plays, can be penetrated by using an off-tackle block by the slot back to influence a defensive false key (See Diagram 2-20).

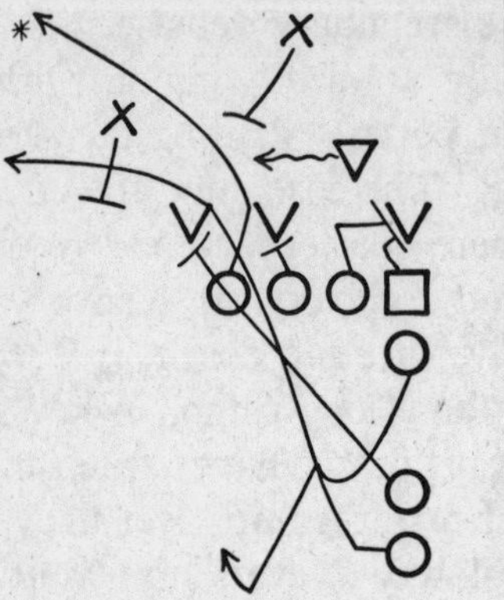

Diagram 2-19 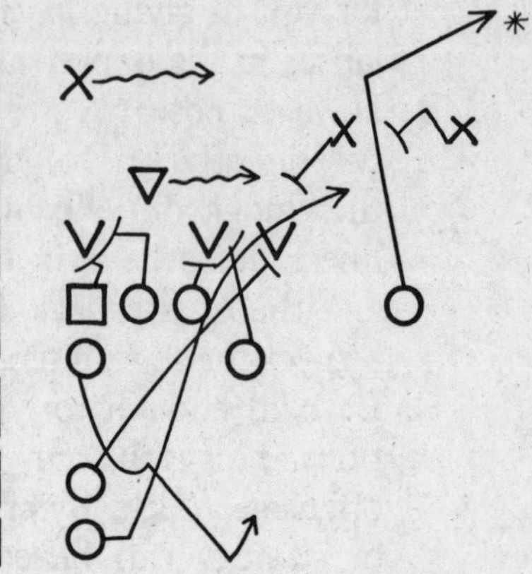   Diagram 2-20

F. Communicate with your field general. There has to be
   a certain rapport between the coach, quarterback and
   receivers, in order to be completely efficient. A feed-
   back of information from the quarterback and the
   receivers to the coach can determine the game's outcome. From this exchange of information, wiser play
   decisions can be made, necessary adjustments can be
   decided upon faster, and, as a fringe benefit, a unified
   belief in what you are trying to accomplish can result
   from this type of communication.

G. Test your opponent's secondary early in the game. Part
   of the objective of the Slot-I's passing attack is to try
   forcing *holes* in the opponent's secondary. Another part
   is to *flood* a coverage area, or simply get a desirable *one-
   on-one* situation in which a talented receiver is mis-
   matched with a less gifted opponent, or to try to get a
   leverage angle between the receiver and the defender,
   and hit the opening. This concept, as illustrated in the
   next chapter, far exceeds ball-control patterns in which
   the offensive ambition is limited to short-gain passes
   into the flats. Our game objectives with the Slot-I
   passing attack, therefore, are these:

   (1) Threaten the long gainer. Make the opponent fear
       run and pass on a fifty-fifty basis.

(2) Create early-game "scare" situations for the defense. If possible, make the opposition psychologically timid. Be willing to apply pressure always and in every way by hitting your opponent with the *unexpected*. Frustration and self-doubt will make your defensive opponent far more vulnerable.

(3) Loosen the defensive pass coverage before stabbing at its front wall. This will help open up running lanes. Your passing attack with the Slot-I is tailored to improve your running game.

(4) Consider going for the "big play" immediately after something bad happens to the opponent, such as a turnover by fumble, or a pass interception.

H. Include the use of formation "wrinkles," that can supplement your passing attack. By making selective use of a Double-Slot formation, slot back "motion," and tailback "fly," an added strain can be placed on the opponent's secondary. Below are some common-sense reasons why such "double width" formation tactics may be helpful.

(1) It is simple to install and use without a loss of time.

(2) It is an excellent means of disengaging a double coverage of your slot-side receivers. (See Diagram 2-21)

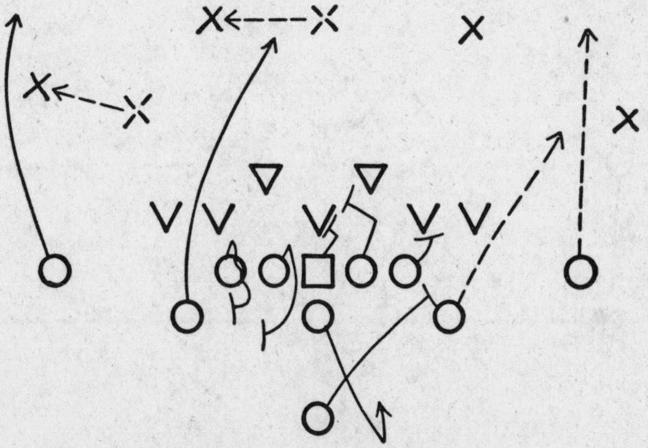

Diagram 2-21 Double Slot

(3) The balance of attack can be strengthened to a given side. (See Diagram 2-22)

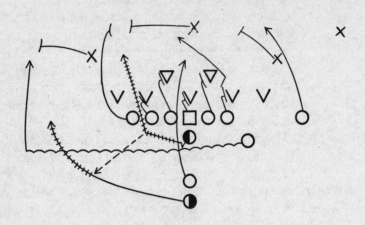

Diagram 2-22 Motion (slot back)

(4) It can make the secondary stretch to its breaking point. (See Diagrams 2-23 and 2-24)

(5) There are a variety of ways to accomplish similar purposes without creating offensive confusion. (See Diagrams 2-25 and 2-26)

(6) It can open up the possibility of clean-breaking hand-offs to the fullback. (See Diagram 2-27)

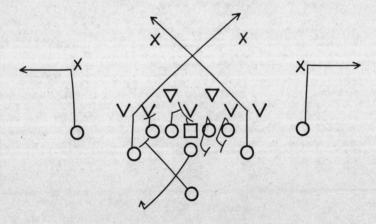

Diagram 2-23 "X" Pattern

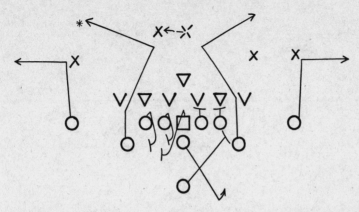

Diagram 2-24 Split Pattern (accredited to former assistant Paul Smith)

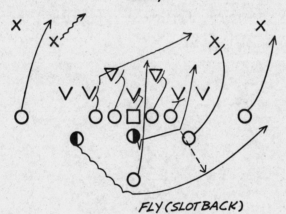

FLY (SLOTBACK)

Diagram 2-25 Base Option

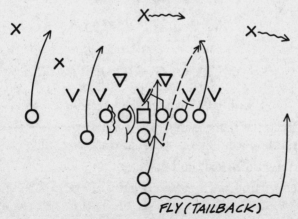

FLY (TAILBACK)

Diagram 2-26 Quick Pass

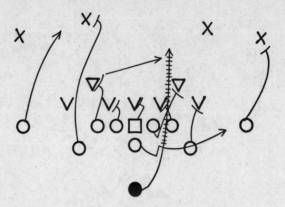

Diagram 2-27 Fullback X-Play

(7) The passing threat is improved and its complementary running game can be retained. (See Diagram 2-28)

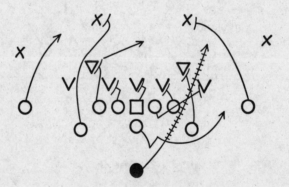

Diagram 2-28 Trap Off-Tackle

SUMMARY OF SLOT-I OBJECTIVES

1. Attack with balance from your offense.
2. Keep the defense in a bind with a specialized power-running side, and a specialized passing side.
3. Attack off-tackle to both sides.
4. Use the forward pass as a basic offensive weapon.

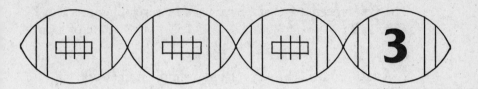

PROCEDURES FOR
DEVELOPING
THE SLOT-I OFFENSE

I have shown you the need for having purposeful objectives in order to use a successful offensive plan of attack; it therefore follows that systematic *procedures* are also necessary in developing and building your offensive system. While a philosophical approach to coaching is an important starting point, it is even more vital that you devise a sound, building, blueprint. Further, your team must master the essential skills and techniques that are consistent with this blueprint and that are also compatible with your players' individual abilities. Consequently, building an efficient offense will be somewhat dependent upon the following considerations:

(1) A plan of operation.

(2) Proper teaching of related fundamentals.

(3) Proper placement of personnel.

(4) Preparatory research.

(5) Continual evaluation and improvement of the overall offensive program.

The procedures used in the development of this Slot-I system come about as a result of love for the above ingredients. Trial and error virtually eliminated other popular offensive systems, whose shortcomings sometimes outweighed their advantages; or else the players were not available to stay with a chosen offense for *consecutive seasons*. Improvements continue to be made with present methods and techniques, but current findings do give this version of the Slot-I offense a complete attack within an adaptable framework.

The five procedures that I have used in developing this Slot-I attack are listed below, followed by a detailed explanation of each.

1. Specialize personnel for efficiency.
2. Attack in different ways, from a simple framework.
3. Develop well-timed pass route cuts.
4. Out-position the defensive perimeter.
5. Wrinkle the offense without changing it.

HOW TO PUT THESE PROCEDURES INTO USE

I. Specialize personnel for efficiency.
  A. *Place your most skilled linemen at the tight side for maximum blocking strength: this will give a strong running game to that side.* At the opposite side, where the defense is forced to defend a strong passing attack, select your slot side linemen for their proficiency in *pass blocking.* About 70 percent of your running plays should normally be run to the tight side. At least 70 percent of the passing action should take place to the slot side. The ability of the Slot-I to make use of personnel placement in this manner is unequaled by any other offensive system.
  B. Make strategic use of flip-flop linemen. Since the basic organization of the offense centers around specialization, flip-flopping is done primarily to: (1) make use of specific player *strengths* and talents at specific positions, (2) explore a mismatch of linemen personnel in favor of the offense, and (3) seek out secondary weaknesses with the two best available receivers used in combination.
  C. Provide enough "cross-over" running plays to the slot side and enough passing plays to the tight side to keep both the offense functional and the defense guessing. By making use of cross-over runs and passes to the side of the least emphasis, the defense can often be hurt from a change-up. Since most of the running game is mirrored to both tight and slot sides, keeping your opponent honest to the running game should never become a problem. Various crossing patterns and the

bootleg pass series are sufficient in keeping the defensive backs at the tight side honest. A play-action quick-pass to the tight end is an easy means of loosening a close secondary rotation at the tight side corner.

D. Apply the following guidelines in placing personnel for the Slot-I:

Tight End—A capable hook blocker for wide plays, a skillful angle blocker for off-tackle plays, and at least a fair receiver. Therefore, a versatile athlete is desirable. His quickness and agility are more important than speed in running pass routes.

Tight Tackle—A physically strong and reliable blocker with a knack for angle blocking. Since he is the centerpoint of the tight side attack, agility and quickness in handling varying blocking situations is helpful. On occasion, he may be asked to pull from the line and lead interference on pitch-outs.

Tight Guard—The best overall lineman on the squad. He should be the stronger, and likely the bigger athlete of the two guards. He should be skilled in double-team blocking with the center on a nose guard. He should be an adequate trap blocker and certainly the better one-on-one blocker of the two guards.

Note: All tight side linemen should be proficient in backside "cup" protection for pull-up and play-action passes.

Center—A reliable performer in snapping the football and blocking a nose guard or middle linebacker. This is important in any team's offense. Quickness is helpful in picking up a linebacker, and adequate size is helpful in protecting your quarterback. Compatibility with the quarterback and intelligence in handling various situations within the defensive middle are plus factors separating the top-flight candidates from the average.

Slot Guard—The quicker of the two guards. He should be very skillful in pass blocking and highly proficient in pulling from the line on various traps, bootlegs, reverses, etc., as he must fulfill this function on misdirection plays.

Slot Tackle—An outstanding pass blocker. He can be the largest and even the slowest athlete on the team, since speed is not essential for the Tackle Trap play. He should be dependable as an angle blocker, and at least fair as a one-on-one blocker of wide plays to his side.

Split End—The best receiver on the team. If available, a *tall* athlete is valuable at this position (many of his routes require a catch to his inside). He should possess good moves, rhythm, and cleverness in catching a football in a crowd.

Slot Back—An athlete who is an exceptional receiver, a fine runner, and who is good on misdirection plays. He can be a small athlete (many of his routes require a catch from inside-out into the flat area). He should be a good open-field runner and one of the best athletes on the team. If his running ability is superior, he can be rotated to tailback on the slot-left formation. A blocking handicap due to physical size can be overcome by adjusting his alignment spacing.

Tailback—A rugged and durable runner, capable of hitting soft spots in the defensive line. Reliability and quickness are necessary, and he should be capable of a quick burst of speed after reaching the line of scrimmage. He should be an average receiver, at least, who could double as a slot back.

Fullback—A solid blocker. As a runner, look for (1) a strong and bullish type, (2) a quick thruster, or (3) an ideal combination of the above, if available.

Quarterback—*First*, a skilled passer who is a competent leader and signal caller. Considerations as to running ability must come second. As the field general, he is required to observe, analyze and exploit. He should have a knack for threatening long-gainer plays, while having the discipline to pilot sustained drives when desirable. He must be capable of throwing timed pass releases to his receivers as their timed route cuts are made. (This is a learning process which requires drilling, patience and personal discipline.) If your quarterback should have running ability, his sprint-out passes, keepers and option plays can be invaluable. (See Diagram 3-1 for a visual recap of personnel placement.)

TIGHT SIDE
70% RUNNING
30% PASSING

SLOT SIDE
70% PASSING
30% RUNNING

GOOD BLOCKER; RECEIVING ABILITY AT LEAST FAIR.
(TE)

STRONG, RELIABLE & AGILE BLOCKER.
(TT)

BEST OVERALL LINEMAN ATHLETE.
(TG)

RELIABLE W/QUICK LEGS.
C

QUICK & ADEPT AT PULLING FROM LINE.
(SG)

GOOD PASS BLOCKER, SIZE IS DESIRABLE.
(ST)

BEST RECEIVER; PREFER A TALL ATHLETE.
(SE)

(Q) GOOD LEADER; PASSER #1 & RUNNER #2.

(SB) NIFTY RUNNER W/GOOD PASS CATCHING HANDS; CAN BE SMALL PHYSICALLY.

SOUND BLOCKER; A QUICK THRUSTER OR STRONG "BULL."
(FB)

(TB) RUGGED & DURABLE RUNNER; CLEVER FOOTWORK A BIG PLUS FACTOR.

Diagram 3-1

Note: If you wish to use your slot back as a tailback in the slot-left formation, a logical relocation of the tailback would be at the left slot position. But if the tailback is not a reliable receiver and the fullback can serve in this capacity, then a rotation of tailback to fullback and fullback to left slot should be considered. This alternative is good, especially if your fullback is a small-but-quick type, and the tailback has a solid physique (See Diagram 3-2).

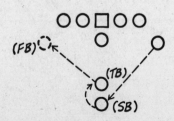

Diagram 3-2

II. Attack in different ways from a simple framework.

A. Apply contrasting pressures upon your opposition's defense by using a variable blocking scheme. A multiple blocking scheme will aid a clever runner in finding his line openings. In contrast, a static blocking system has a greater likelihood of being stymied by good defensive football teams.

B. Teach cut-back footwork to all your running backs so that a premature defensive penetration can be overcome, if and when it occurs. An I-formation running back can compensate for a blocking miscue by an offensive lineman, because his centralized running angle is well-suited to an immediate running adjustment. By taking advantage of the balance offered by a tandem alignment, clever footwork by the tailback or fullback can be the winning difference when facing an overanxious or over-committing defense.

C. Make full use of sudden, quick strikes into the line. To be completely efficient, the fullback Base play should simultaneously strike off-center as the blocking linemen are making their contact. Good explosion by your offensive linemen and fullback can get three yards: good follow-through will get a larger gain! The depth of your fullback is important in achieving this split-second strike.

D. Include the necessary offensive tools that can help keep the opponent's defense loose and in a state of confusion.

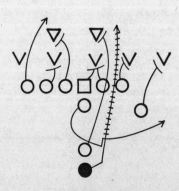

Diagram 3-3

1. *Prod Alignment Weaknesses:* Your purpose is to seek out the "soft spots" that exist in all defensive alignments (See Diagram 3-3).
2. *Vary Line Spacings:* Your purpose is to widen individual defenders on inside runs, and to tighten the defensive front on wide runs (See Diagram 3-4).

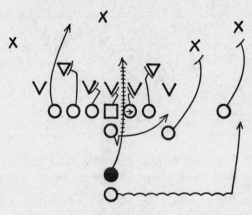

Diagram 3-4

3. *Develop Precision Counters:* Your purpose is to explore the reaction keys of the defense with well-timed counter-measures (See Diagram 3-5).

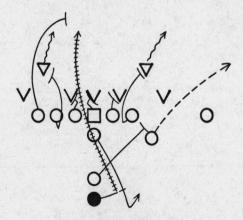

Diagram 3-5

4. *Exploit Trapping:* Your purpose is to gain blocking angles, enhance play-fakes and destroy zealous

penetration by defensive linemen (See Diagram 3-6).

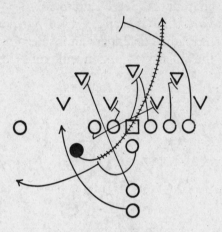

Diagram 3-6

5. *Apply Angle and Double-Team Blocking:* Your purpose is to seal off pursuit at the point of attack (See Diagram 3-7).

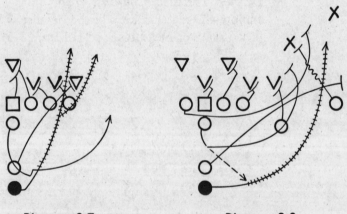

Diagram 3-7   **Diagram 3-8**

6. *Perfect Sweep Blocking:* Your purpose is to develop a quick-striking wide play that has ample running room up the sideline (See Diagram 3-8).
7. *Include Optioning:* Your purpose is to gain an advantage of running-lane choices at a perimeter breakdown area (See Diagram 3-9).

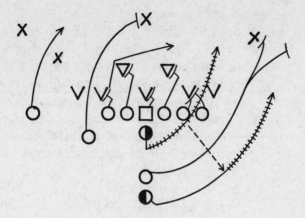

Diagram 3-9

III. Develop well-timed pass-route cuts.
  A. Design pass patterns with at least two receivers within your quarterback's direct line of view. This two-receiver pattern arrangement is designated as the quarterback's first option. If your quarterback fakes the off-tackle Power play prior to his pass release, a third receiver from the backfield may also appear in his line of view. By having two, and possibly three, receivers in *direct view* for the first option, your quarterback can make an intelligent selection of his available choices and do a better job in coping with multiple pass coverages that may be used by the opposing defensive secondary (See Diagram 3-10).

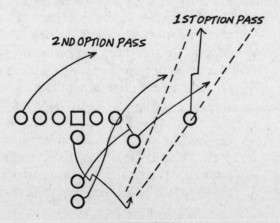

Diagram 3-10

1. Quarterback requisites:
   a. Set up quickly at a depth of 2-9 yards on pull-up passes. Your pocket-depth is determined by the military beats of the pattern break, which is pre-called in the huddle. (The military beat system was influenced by Coach Frank Kush during a Louisiana High School Coaches Association clinic.) The time-beat required for the quarterback's pull-up is always one count *before* the receiver's route break. With play-action passes, a fullback fake is often used with a 3-beat route break, while a tailback fake is used with a 4-beat count. Sprint-out passes may use a 5-beat route break, with the quarterback throwing on his own timing.
      (1) *2-beat count:* A quick, 2 yard pocket-release on the first beat.
      (2) *3-beat count:* An approximate 5 yard pocket-release on the second beat.
      (3) *4-beat count:* A *normal* 6-7 yard pocket-release behind the tackle on the third beat.
      (4) *5-beat count:* An extended 8-9 yard pocket-release on the fourth beat.
   b. When pulling-up, discipline yourself to get your feet planted in the pass pocket with shoulders squared to the scrimmage line and release the football quickly on the designated time-beat.
   c. Communicate with your receivers in working out adjustments with their time-beats for all team patterns during game competition.
   d. Shorten your time-beat for pull-up passes if you are pressured by defensive blitzes, or else elect to throw from a sprint-out to evade internal defensive pressures. You will find that a time-beat passing attack is considerably more efficient, precise and flexible than those methods which attempt to correlate the quarterback's pocket depth to that of his receivers' upfield distance or

the number of steps taken prior to their final route break.

2. Receiver requisites:

   a. Make a sharp break on your final route cut in accordance to the time-beat count given in the huddle. The yard depth for each route will vary in proportion to the individual speed, maturity and stride length of each receiver. Variations will therefore occur with each receiver. The depth of a route can be shortened or lengthened by changing the coordinated passer-receiver time-beat of a pass pattern.

      (1) *2-beat count*—A quick, 5 yard angle-in or route break.

      (2) *3-beat count*—An approximate 7-9 yard cut.

      (3) *4-beat count*—A *normal* 12-15 yard cut.

      (4) *5-beat count*—An extended 18-25 yard final cut.

   b. Discipline yourself to make your final route break on the designated time-beat given in the huddle.

   c. Advise the quarterback of your needs in making a time-beat adjustment which can help you break clean on specified patterns.

B. Instruct the quarterback to pivot toward his second receiver group, if and when he rejects the receiver choices in his first-option. The time-beat concept is abandoned in the mechanics of locating the second option. From a regular, single-slot formation, only one receiver will appear in the second option with a pass thrown from the slot side pocket.

1. If an offensive back is deployed in "fly" or "motion," or in a Double-Slot formation, there may be two receivers found in the second option. Their locations, however, may be less centralized than the receivers found in the first option-receiver group.

C. Emphasize to your quarterback the importance of throwing on instinct. The principle of the first and second option is very simple to apply, and there is no need to go through a chain of mental decisions.

1. When neither option appears open, however, your quarterback should be preinstructed to do one of the following things:
   a. Throw the football out of bounds, or
   b. Run for any clearance, taking the ball out of bounds if the clock needs to be stopped.

D. Take advantage of the special blocking reinforcement that a tandem backfield can give. This resource is available from the Slot-I system without a loss of simplicity. Below are some of the flexible steps that you can take in order to adjust to varying pass/rush situations.

1. The tight end could be called upon to "stay at home" and give added blocking security to the backside cup protection on certain slot side pocket passes (See Diagram 3-11).

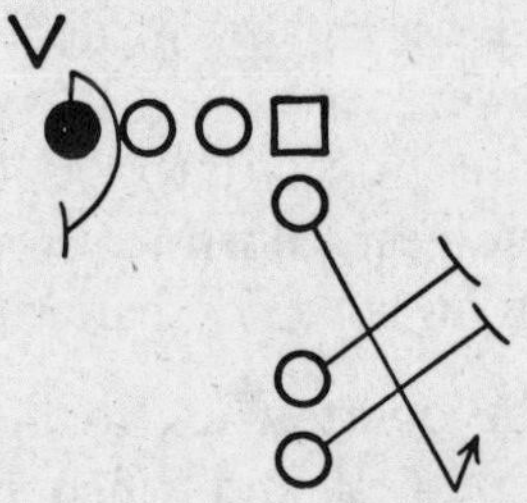

Diagram 3-11

2. From a pull-up pass, the fullback can be used to pick up an anticipated middle blitz when facing a 5-3 type defense. By his normal assignment, the tailback would block the playside defensive end (See Diagram 3-12).

3. The tailback can be invaluable as a backside blocker while the fullback blocks the play-side defensive end (See Diagram 3-13).

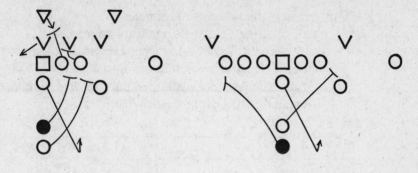

Diagram 3-12   **Diagram 3-13**

4. The tailback also can be used as an inside "area" blocker, while the fullback takes the outside blocking assignment. If the fullback is your best blocker, his prowess can be used to contain a tough defensive end (See Diagram 3-14).

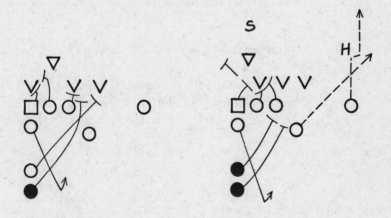

Diagram 3-14   **Diagram 3-15**

5. A hard corner or "overload" defense, such as a Split-6, can be blocked with your regular backfield blocking assignments: the fullback blocks the first defender outside his offensive tackle, while the tailback blocks his outermost defender, who is the defensive end (See Diagram 3-15).

IV. Out-position the defensive perimeter.
   A. Use stretching principles against a zone:
      1. *A Vertical Stretch*—Involves expansion of a zone deep, either to break it down or to empty it so that a trail receiver can be dumped into the void you have created (See Diagram 3-16).

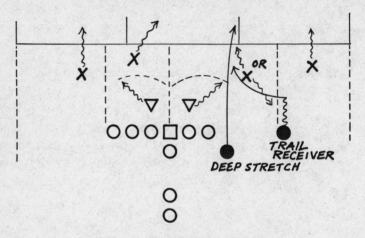

Diagram 3-16 A Vertical Stretch

      2. *A Horizontal Stretch*—Involves expansion of a zone defense sideways, thereby breaking it down at its seams and underneath the linebacker areas (See Diagram 3-17).

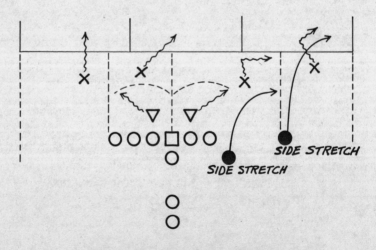

Diagram 3-17 A Horizontal Stretch

3. *A Combination Vertical and Horizontal Stretch*—
   Involves a blending of pass cuts which can put a
   strain on defensive perimeter coverages, both deep
   and wide. You have unlimited possibilities for
   developing pattern combinations with this theory.
   a. The central idea is to create holes within a zone
      defense by jockeying defenders into over-ex-
      tended coverage positions. The "stretch" con-
      cept has been used to some extent on the college
      level and by professional football leagues at a
      time when zone defenses began to restrict the
      traditional, man-to-man oriented pass-offenses
      (See Diagram 3-18).

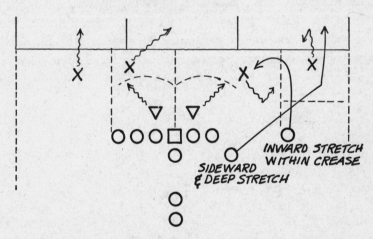

Diagram 3-18 A Combination Vertical and Horizontal Stretch

   b. Penetration into the "underneath" zone-areas
      can be exploited best by your tight end, since he
      is the logical receiver to slip into any openings
      that occur when the secondary doubles up on
      your slot side receivers, prerotates, or "rolls up"
      into that side. Your tight end will find his best
      clearing whenever the inside linebackers use
      extreme "fall-back" measures to contain the
      threat of a deep pass.
   c. Single coverage situations that may result when a
      zone defense is being "stretched" can be at-
      tacked in much the same way as man coverage.

Either out-position the opponent with a sharp cut, at a prescribed distance, or attain a desirable angle (leverage) between the defender and the passer.

B. Gain leverage on pass defenders:

1. The strategy is to attain a position between the defender and the passer that would make a pass interception unlikely. This applies to *any* one-on-one situation.

2. Outside leverage implies that an outward angle has been achieved, to the advantage of the receiver. This angle gives your passer a safe delivery of the football between the sideline and his receiver.

3. Inside leverage implies that an inward angle has been achieved by a receiver, between the passer and the defender, hopefully avoiding the inside linebackers (See Diagram 3-19 for an illustration of a combined inside and outside leverage).

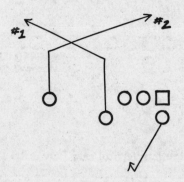

Diagram 3-19 Outside Leverage (#1) and Inside Leverage (#2)

4. The means of gaining a leverage advantage on pass defenders are numerous.

a. Drive the defender deep using preliminary feints, then take a sharp cut to the assigned side. A combination of cuts can also be made, as in the case of a snake route. These calculated maneuvers are effective against man coverage, as well as single coverage within a zone (See Diagram 3-20).

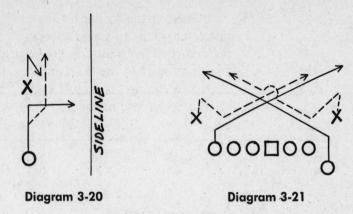

Diagram 3-20   Diagram 3-21

    b. Use crossing receivers as a means to crowd man coverage at the junction point and to gain that important outside position with the opponent (See Diagram 3-21).

    c. Use play-action fakes to freeze the overall perimeter, as an aid in helping your receivers achieve a one-on-one relationship within zone areas, thus giving opportune cuts with inside or outside leverage (See Diagram 3-22).

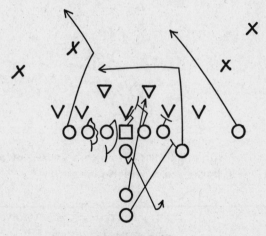

Diagram 3-22

    d. Use a tailback "fly" and slotback "motion" as a means of gaining leverage by causing secondary adjustments.

(1) A rotation of the secondary may result in a mismatch with its single coverage on your favored receiver. This can give the receiver an opportunity to use fakes and cuts into an open area having a desirable angle (See Diagram 3-23 for two methods).

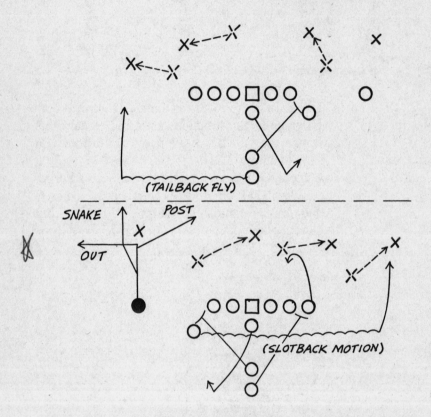

Diagram 3-23 Possible Rotation Mismatches Caused by a Fly-Back (above) and a Motion-Back (below)

(2) A rotation of the secondary toward the tight side can give a leverage advantage to your backside receivers as they angle inward, which is opposite the defensive rotation. An example of this backside phenomenon will

follow in section C, which concerns zone-
defense flooding.
C. Flood the pockets in a zone defense:
   1. *With Play-Action*—Use the tailback to flood a zone
      by slipping him out of the backfield after a running
      play-fake. Play-action helps freeze linebacker reac-
      tions so the opponent can be outnumbered within a
      zone. This is accomplished by sending out more
      receivers in a specific area than the immediate
      defenders can cover. Play-action passes from a Slot-
      I give *added diversity* in placing pressure on the
      defense, by using the identical patterns of the pull-
      up series, without a change in timing (See Diagram
      3-24).

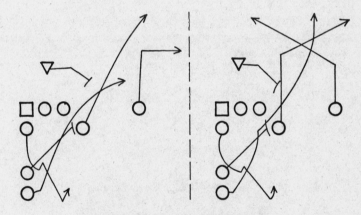

Diagram 3-24 Play-Action Freeze

   2. *With a Fly-Back*—Use a tailback "fly," before the
      snap of the football, to add an extra receiver at the
      tight side sideline and to stretch the secondary
      laterally (See Diagram 3-25).
   3. *With a Motion-Back*—Use a slot-back "motion"
      prior to the ball snap, in conjunction with a bootleg
      pass series, for the purpose of flooding the tight
      side sideline. This should be a planned part of the
      necessary tight side passing threat (See Diagram
      3-26).

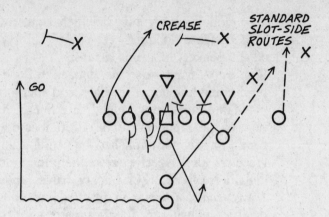

Diagram 3-25 Fly-Back Receiver

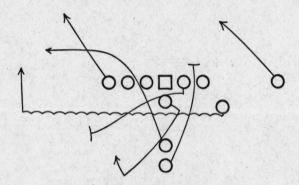

Diagram 3-26 Motion-Back Receiver

4. *With a Double-Slot Plus Motion*—Use a slot-back "motion" from a four-receiver formation, giving an effective flood of receivers opposite the pull-up pocket. This is an excellent means of breaking up special rotations and double coverages. A backside flood pattern is more difficult to defend than an obvious onside flood. Your receiver's route rules are simple.

   a. The onside split end runs a pre-called route ("Out," "Snake" or "Post").

   b. The motion-back takes a straight-up route after clearing outside the end.

   c. The remaining backside receivers run a simple angle-in course, each dividing their crease deep to their inside. The throwing distance to any selected receiver is within the range of an average quarterback (See Diagram 3-27).

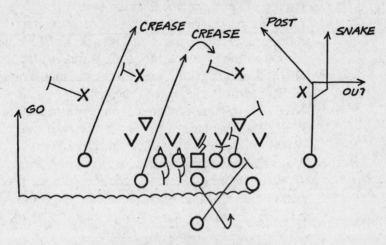

Diagram 3-27 Backside Flood

V. Wrinkle the offense without changing it.
  A. Set standard guidelines for your formation variations.
    1. *"Wrinkle without change"*—a sound motto for you to adopt for each and every football season.
      a. Vary in such a way that your formation play-structure is not affected drastically.
      b. If a play series is taught to a specific side, either tight side or slot side, this should remain much the same when you move into a variation of your formation. To do otherwise may destroy the simplicity that a flip-flop system offers.
      c. Your advantage with a formation wrinkle concept is that play calls will not change sides in most cases, although an alignment variation may eliminate certain plays or pass patterns within designated areas.
    2. Make the defense overextend itself at its alignment weakness with your basic offense. Sometimes the opponent, when forced to adjust, may reveal a new weakness.
    3. Keep your offensive system flexible, but simple. With a full understanding of the internal operations

of your overall offense, you can exercise flexibility without losing a sense of direction. If an innovation fits into your offensive system, then use it. If it is foreign to your system, then reject it.

4. Make formation variations a part of your practice routine *after* the basic Slot-I attack has become second nature to your athletes. Continually practice all fundamental skills and formation innovations through drills functional to the game.

5. Keep your offense economical but compatible with itself. An advantage of the Slot-I offense is that its plays complement themselves in series.

6. Maintain a mental picture of the keystone offense in all your planning, so that variations can be used without losing a sense of direction. A common coaching cliche is "What you do may not be right OR wrong—but it is what you do!"

   a. Every championship team has a "heart" within its overall offense no matter how diversified that team may appear. When the going gets tough, high caliber teams will invariably come back to the things they believe in.

   b. The Slot-I can threaten with great variety, while staying within its keystone framework. First the offense must have a solid foundation of well-executed plays. Wrinkles can always be added to expand the base of operation. You should remember that basics, not frills, cause a winning team's performance.

   c. A special play or two can be easily included in game preparation, to give your offense an element of surprise without upsetting formation-play balance. Your precaution should not be in a use of special plays so much as in attempting to put in a large number of plays one week, only to throw it all out the next week for another formation and set of plays.

d. The point of emphasis is this: your team must rely upon whatever it can execute best. Offensive plays are a team's weapons, while formations serve as the tools which can keep the game from becoming an equation of manpower superiority.

B. Safeguard against the drawbacks of over-innovation.

1. Avoid the temptation to swap horses at midstream with any part of your offensive system. If a season takes a slow start, use caution and reluctance in making a change in your core system. Modify when necessary, but do not overhaul your entire offense once the season starts!

2. Avoid the temptation to "borrow" from other coaches *without* regard to your own material. Another coach's "muscle offense," for example, may be *his* salvation but *your* downfall.

3. Avoid the temptation to use a myriad of formations with pet-play tendencies. A fragmentary offense usually lacks continuity: its scattered pieces, borrowed from other systems, often have formation tendencies and can be highly predictable. Wrinkling from a set offense, in contrast, can *prevent* a change in play-call balance or a loss of execution. On occasion, additional alignments should be used to aid offensive continuity, providing these alignments are compatible with this concept of wrinkling from a set offense.

a. A loosened "flex" of the slot back from his normal 1-yard split can give him unobstructed releases off the line, can create man-coverage situations upon an inverted secondary, and can place a lateral strain upon the coverage of a 3-deep zone perimeter. A disadvantage of using a flexed formation full-time is that much of its running-play authority, off-tackle, is lost to the slot side against some defensive alignments, while slot-back misdirection plays either are weakened or eliminated (See Diagram 3-28).

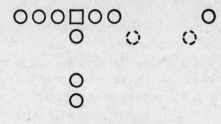

Diagram 3-28

b. A tight-slot adjustment by the split end can make possible a double-team blocking combination, which is ideally suited for a power-sweep play. With the split end assuming a 2-yard spacing from the slot back, a different pass-release angle must be covered by the defensive secondary. Also, a weak-arm quarterback could benefit from his close receivers. If a halfback shift is made by the tailback into a Slot-T set, certain plays can be used to hit more directly into the line. If you depart from the regular Slot-I for supplemental reasons, but wish to keep a centralized fullback, it is my opinion that the Slot-T is the most compatible alternative, since a 4-back running game persists while misdirection plays and slot side pass patterns are, for the most part, retained. A disadvantage of using a tight slot full time is that the defensive secondary is not forced to spread at either corner, and there is a loss of "mirror play" simplicity. Also, from a halfback set, many of the tailback and fullback assignments must be interchanged because of the backfield shift. The fullback would run the Isolate and Power plays; therefore, the tailback is removed from his role of a fluid runner to both sides of the line (See Diagram 3-29).

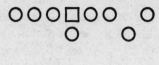

Diagram 3-29

c. A Slot-Veer wrinkle can add a twin-dive feature to the Slot-I's play format, by exploiting instantaneous ball handling along the line of scrimmage. Since a veer (triple) option can be executed in a very simple manner from a split backfield, as explained in Chapter 10, less emphasis needs to be placed on an off-tackle attack which gives opportunity to split both ends and flex the slot back as needed. From this double-width alignment, mirror play and counter-action benefits are retained, while the defensive corners are pressured with containing both the option and passing game. A disadvantage of using a Slot-Veer full time, is that centralized running angles are non-existent for either running back, and each must qualify as strong inside runners, as well as explosive outside runners on the option pitch. Then, too, the quarterback should possess an adeptness to run options and command respect with his passing arm (See Diagram 3-30).

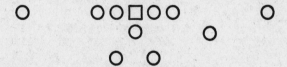

Diagram 3-30

CLOSING REMARKS

As coach, whatever decisions you make in your offensive planning, it is imperative that you decide first what is the *single best thing* going for you in the upcoming season! Then you must spend all available time working on its development. You can never afford to become enslaved to your past traditions and accomplishments. Personnel weaknesses and injury possibilities always have to be taken into account, so that your building foundation will remain solid for the duration of the season.

SUMMARY OF SLOT-I PROCEDURES

1. Specialize personnel for efficiency.
2. Attack in different ways from a simple framework.
3. Develop well-timed pass-route cuts.
4. Out-position the defensive perimeter.
5. Wrinkle the offense without changing it.

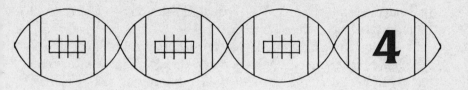

SIMPLIFYING
BLOCKING FUNDAMENTALS
FOR THE SLOT-I

To win, a team must have *blocking!* With an ability to move obstacles out of the way, scoring will take care of itself.

Quickness is an important element in any sport if superiority is to be gained over the opposition. Quickness in football concerns getting an edge over your opponent. The lighter the athlete, the more necessary this "edge" becomes. One of the main advantages the offense has over the defense is its opportunity to get off together on the snap of the ball. In blocking, beating your opponent to the punch is essential to victory.

HOW TO TEACH CUT-OFF BLOCKING

Cut-off blocking is a necessity to the success of a Slot-I formation. The Slot-I's tandem backfield can fully realize its centralized running advantage when blocking contact at the line of scrimmage can stop defensive penetration, keep the neutral zone in check, and tie-up pursuit. Stiff competition has influenced us to combine angle blocking patterns with cut-off blocking techniques, to improve our offensive advantage at the point of attack.

Sound cut-off blocking technique begins with the fundamentals of a well-drilled *shoulder block*. The blocker should be taught to use a "bull" neck in forming a neck-shoulder "V" during initial contact with his cut-off side shoulder. A neck-shoulder wedge at the cut-off side will help shut off his opponent's line of pursuit.

We like to teach a *scramble block* technique as well, to offer each blocker other alternatives such as (1) a play-side changeup, (2) a backside seal-off, or (3) a second-effort response to a loss of shoulder contact with the defender.

After acquiring a fundamental background in shoulder and scramble blocking, varying tactics can be added, in combat situations, to include: (1) a low crotch charge to tie up the defender's legs, (2) a lunge-and-crab charge to achieve a reverse hook of the blocker's hip, (3) a reach-and-hook charge to help gain an outside cut-off position on a loose-playing defender, (4) a false-step charge to influence the defender into making a mistaken play-diagnosis, and (5) a high chest charge to wall off the pursuit angle of a soft-playing opponent, a technique that is also used in pass protection.

As various blocking situations arise, it is practical to have more than one basic blocking approach at your linemen's disposal. The concept of cut-off blocking is intended to intermix strategy with application, by making use of the related blocking styles of both shoulder and scramble techniques.

APPLICATION

Stance:

1. Take a balanced 3-point stance, feet parallel, and spread to the width of the shoulders. Your toes, heels and thighs should be in a straight line. Never lean or point your stance.
2. Place weight on balls of feet and extend fingers of your strong arm on the turf. Your middle fingers of the down hand should be placed in a tripod with slight forward pressure to improve take-off.
3. Maintain a flat back with head and eyes up for proper spring. Keep eyes always on the blocking target. Mobility and leg power begin with a good stance.
4. If your right hand is grounded, the left forearm should lay ready on your left knee.

Uncoil:

1. "Bull" your neck for strength, stability and safety.
2. Get leg intensity. Be ready to spring out before the snap cadence begins.
3. Concentrate on beating your opponent to the punch! You should always be mentally ready, determined and eager as you prepare to uncoil from your stance.

4. Fire-out on the snap signal with cat-like quickness.

5. Explode hard off the nearside foot, and fire your head through the cut-off point, splitting the opponent from the play hole or sealing off his gap charge.

6. With neck "bulled," strike the defender solidly with your cut-off side shoulder. If you wish to scramble block your opponent, you should aim just above the defender's knee at the cut-off side. With a shoulder block, aim at the opponent's armpit at the cut-off side and jolt him back with your initial contact.

7. Concentrate on your quickness of release to prevent the opposition from penetrating across the line, or from making a "quick read" reaction to the play flow.

8. Strike from a low, inclining angle, with a bend in your knees. If blocking a linebacker, go at him from an anticipated interception point with quick, driving steps. Guard against an overextension of your legs: this is a common fault in a loss of blocking contact.

9. When angle-blocking a linebacker from outside-in, it first may be *necessary* to step into the nearby defensive lineman with your outside foot and break his charge! This can be accomplished by slamming your outside shoulder pad underneath the opponent's inside pad and *turning him outward* before attempting to inside-step toward the anticipated collision point with the linebacker.

Follow Through:

FOR SHOULDER BLOCK

1. Make a sharp, brisk contact with your cut-off side shoulder. Then follow-up with the flippers, snapping them up from underneath. This will give a legal, one-two punch on your initial contact.

2. Keep your head locked in a straight line with your back. A curved back and turned head indicate poor technique, which invites injury.

3. Make contact snugly between your headgear and shoulder pad, with forearms up. The opponent should be locked within the "V" of your neck-shoulder blocking surface. Never hit on the point of the shoulder.

4. Follow through instantaneously with quick, driving steps on the balls of the feet. Take care to work your tail around so body position can be achieved between the opponent and ball carrier. Use your head as a steering post, preventing penetration and controlling the movements of your assigned defender. Never quit working your feet while the play is live.

FOR SCRAMBLE BLOCK

1. Fight your inside hand to the ground instantly, as contact is made just above the opponent's knee at the cut-off side.
2. Then go immediately to all-fours in a scramble, and *work your head and tail upfield*! Never falter between body contact and your follow-up scramble.
3. Scramble *through* the defender, keeping your shoulder pad pressed snugly into his legs. Do not lose your momentum by trying to hook the opponent. It is also important that you not lose your opponent from the rear, thus giving him an advantageous pursuit angle to the ball carrier.
4. Remember, you should end the game with dirty hands—not dirty britches.

ADDITIONAL BLOCKING POINTERS

1. The success of a cut-off block begins with ...
   (a) Proper stance, consisting of a wide foot-base.
   (b) Intense anticipation and a desire to excel.
   (c) Quickness of release from your stance.
   (d) Getting under the opponent's charge with an explosive dip.
   (e) A broad contact surface, squaring-up your body after contact.
   (f) Churning footwork during your follow-through, with a burning desire to out-hustle your opponent.
2. Your leg intensity and instant explosion with the ball snap are more important than physical size.
3. Always sustain contact, unless an acrossfield or screen pass-block is assigned.

4. Your follow-through technique is simply an execution of leg drive mixed with fanatical effort.

5. Quickness, technique and precision can be developed with a few extra minutes of daily work on a blocking sled. Do extra work on sled uncoils with your "weak" shoulder, ensuring that a squared-up position is kept as you explode outward.

6. To become an outstanding blocker, begin developing your reflexes, leg spring and physical strength during the off-season. Participate in quickness, jumping and resistive exercises in a planned routine, at home or at school. If you neglect to develop yourself during the off-season, you will have no one but *yourself* to blame later.

COMBINATION AND SPECIAL BLOCKS FOR LINEMEN

Team blocking patterns require the offense linemen to apply various combination and special blocks to comply with their blocking assignments, and to cope with unusual defensive fronts. The techniques that were described in the coverage of cut-off blocking will apply, likewise, to all combination and special blocks.

The placement of the blocker's headgear is an all-important coaching point. Since the defense can pose either a read-and-react or a penetrate-and-react situation, there also should be two guidelines used to determine the appropriate angle for a blocker to fire his head and shoulder. In most cases, a blocker should think in terms of firing his headgear to the side that will *split his opponent from the play hole*. But there are instances when a *gap cut-off* must take its precedence in stopping a defender's intention to penetrate into the offensive backfield. In a gap cut-off situation, the blocker must fire his headgear and shoulder pad *across* the attack hole to subdue a penetration danger.

In the following explanations of combination and special blocks, illustrations will clarify their meaning and purpose. Note the suggested position of headgear placement at the point of cut-off.

Gap Combo:

This block is used when the defense lines up in its front-wall trenches. Each blocker should attempt to seal off penetration with a gap cut-off charge and drive his opponent inward. When facing a gapped interior, the center should block high to the play-side, while his onside guard blocks their mutual opponent with a low block (See Diagram 4-1).

Diagram 4-1

Loop Block:

This block is used when blocking a stack defense. The blocker *nearest* the point of attack is assigned to block the stacked *linebacker*; the blocker *away* from the point of attack must reach-step and cut the charge of the stack lineman. This rule is applicable to gap, head-up and offset stacks (See Diagram 4-2).

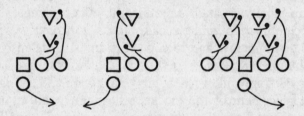

Diagram 4-2

Reach-and-Hook Block:

This block is used primarily by the tight end on wide plays to his side. A reach-and-hook block consists of a standard shoulder block, with the blocker attemtping to reach-step for outside position. If he can stretch outward for a favorable outside position, he can then hook his head while pivoting his buttocks to the outside. He will then use his elongated body to achieve a cut-off advantage (See Diagram 4-3).

Diagram 4-3

Pull-Out Blocks:

Various pull-out blocks are used in situations when a pulling lineman is called upon to block a defensive end, lead interference around the corner, trap a forceful defensive lineman or set up a wall for a screen pass.

Lead—Used by a pulling lineman when a defender must be blocked for bootleg passes, sweeps and, on occasion, outside reverses. On a bootleg (Waggle), the guard is instructed to aim his charge just outside the opponent's farside jersey number, and to follow through without interruption while on the run (See Diagram 4-4).

Diagram 4-4

Trap—Used by an offensive tackle or guard when trapping in the middle and off-tackle. The blocking approach is always made from an inside-out angle. Refer to Chapter 5 for blocking assignments and guidelines which apply to a variety of defensive structures.

Double Team:

This block is used primarily on Lead Option, Isolate, Isolate Keep or Option, and Tackle Trap plays. The inside blocker's function is to stalemate his opponent as the outside blocker drives him backward and away from the point of attack. A modern refinement of this blocking method is to instruct the inside blocker to cut-off block his opponent as if he were not to receive any help. The drive man then becomes a clean-up blocker who walls-off the area, and can bump-off if not needed to seek out a loose linebacker (See Diagram 4-5).

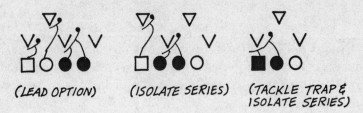

(LEAD OPTION)   (ISOLATE SERIES)   (TACKLE TRAP & ISOLATE SERIES)

Diagram 4-5

Fold and Cross Blocks:

These blocking combinations are used when two offensive blockers gain an advantage by swapping assignments. Normally the outside blocker "blocks down" on his inside defender, while the inside blocker takes a drop-step backward and X-blocks his partner's assigned defender. A variation to this blocking sequence can be found in a Y-block: whereby, the inside blocker goes first and the outside blocker goes second, a tactic useful sometimes on counter-action plays. In a fold-back situation against a Split-4 (6) defense, the onside tackle is required to cut off gap penetration as his companion guard folds from behind to pick up the inside linebacker (See Diagram 4-6).

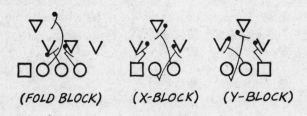

(FOLD BLOCK)   (X-BLOCK)   (Y-BLOCK)

Diagram 4-6

Screen—Used when setting up a screen-pass wall. Assignments: tackle, kick out the defensive halfback if he advances toward the line of scrimmage; guard, set up a wall inside the tackle's block and use zone blocking; center, pull out and curl back to pick up any backside drift. As the blocking wall is formed, an area-blocking rule is applied by the three linemen in the screen wall. Shoulder blocking techniques are recommended (See Diagram 4-7).

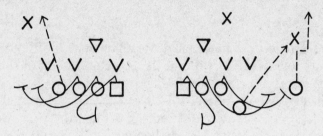

Diagram 4-7

Wedge Block:

Wedge blocking is primarily used on our quarterback sneak ("Goose") play. A blocking wedge is very effective against a waiting defense and can be used as a goal line and short-yardage offense in itself, especially if combined with a fullback plunge. All normal blocking rules are ignored and are replaced by an inside area-blocking principle. All interior linemen, plus the tight end and slot back, must fire out on the snap of the football and lock their inside shoulders with their innermost teammate's shoulder pads. Each blocker's elbows should fit snugly under the armpit of his inside partner. The center serves as the apex man against a 5-man front, and the tight guard becomes the apex on a 6-man front. The seven wedging blockers charge in unison, without allowing any gaps to open from the blocker's inside. All linemen explode off the line with high chest blocking. If the wedging blockers manage to force their opponents to raise upward, the momentum of the massive blocking force can pave the way for a sizeable gain (See Diagram 4-8).

Diagram 4-8

Acrossfield Block:

Acrossfield blocking is taught to all lineman for backside play use. After initial contact with the defensive opponent, the backside tackle releases from the line and takes a shallow course to the immediate play-hole area. He is instructed to seek out the first foreign jersey that approaches, come under control with a widened foot-base and block with a "bulled neck." A running-shoulder block has proven itself the most practical. The backside guard and center should take "delayed cover" to aid the ball carrier, once the line of scrimmage has been crossed (See Diagram 4-9).

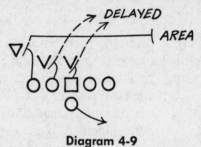

Diagram 4-9

BLOCKING METHODS FOR ENDS AND SLOT BACK

When not assigned to base-blocking duties, the ends and slot back have a primary task of "forcing" the perimeter deep at the play-side and slicing its creases from the backside. The split end has an additional assignment to shield block an inverted safety or outside linebacker on off-tackle and wide plays to his side.

Force:

When a play-side receiver is assigned to release upfield, he is responsible for driving his secondary defender backward on the pretense of a full-speed pass route, then break-down into hitting position with blocking leverage kept between the opponent and the sideline. The idea is to force the secondary to cover-pass, and then stalk the nearby defender away from the running lane. When facing a pass-oriented offense such as the Slot-I, the defense must honor all receiver releases upfield or else face the possible consequences of a fatal touchdown pass-reception (Diagram 4-10).

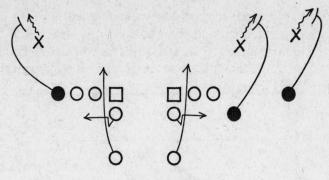

Diagram 4-10

Crease:

Each backside receiver is instructed to run the *seam* between his two nearest secondary defenders in the vicinity of the play. This tactic is used to take two defenders into the deep secondary from the backside, and to analyze weaknesses in the opposition's pass coverage. After the play is recognized by the secondary defense as a run, each backside receiver should stalk his closest challenger and prevent his clean recovery in pursuit of the ball carrier. The slot back should be conscious of containing the #2 defender from the outside (strong safety). (Diagram 4-11).

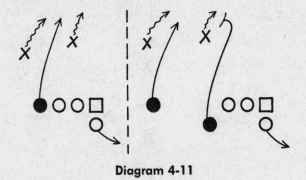

Diagram 4-11

Shield:

A shield block is assigned to a split end, on wide runs to his side. This blocking technique is a cautious version of a crack-back block. The split receiver approaches the inverted safety or outside linebacker with deliberation, breaks down his stance into hitting position before contact, then stalks his opponent. A high chest block is used and contact is never made while the opponent's back is turned (See Diagram 4-12).

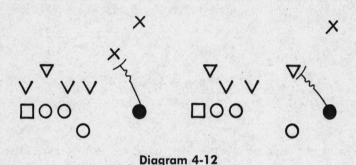

Diagram 4-12

Switch:

A switch is a combo block of the split end and slot back, in which blocking assignments are swapped on designated option plays. A switch call is a useful change-up in short-yardage situations, and also when difficulty is experienced in executing normal forcing tactics. The split end uses a shield block on the inverted safety or outside linebacker, as the slot back releases to angle-block the defensive halfback into the sideline (See Diagram 4-13).

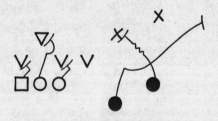

Diagram 4-13

Cut:

A cut is a running shoulder-block used by the slot back, when blocking an outside linebacker or defensive end from a wide (flex) alignment. A widened spacing of the slot back sometimes aids his pass-route releases off the scrimmage line, and may give a beneficial cut-blocking angle on wide plays against alignment adjustments made by the defense (See Diagram 4-14).

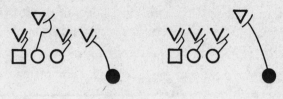

Diagram 4-14

BLOCKING TECHNIQUES FOR RUNNING BACKS

Although the fullback is the premier blocker in a Slot-I backfield, all backs should become proficient in blocking since their services are necessary at various times. An unselfish offensive backfield that consists of athletes who will block for each other, will win its share of football games. As for the Slot-I fullback, his dedicated blocking services are vital to the basic function of the offense and his successful performance should receive timely praise. In the following breakdown, you will find a safe and sure means of teaching efficiency in blocking that will stimulate player involvement and team harmony.

Climb Block:

This block is used by the fullback against linebackers on lead and isolation plays, and against defensive ends on off-tackle and pass-protection plays. A climb block is used by the tailback on any keeper plays after his faking is completed, and also on pass-protection plays. For the tailback to get his full running benefit from a fullback's climb block at the attack point, he must cut opposite the momentum of the block.

The objective of a climb block, therefore, is to tie-up the challenger so that the runner can have leeway in breaking for daylight. A smaller athlete can dominate a larger athlete momentarily, by making use of a proper approach angle, and by climbing up into the defender's face during the follow-through. A prolonged tie-up can be achieved by the blocker making an effort to drive his headgear through the cut-off point, and then follows up with a subsequent rotation of his hips and feet.

Pointers...

1. Step from a balanced stance with your nearside foot, and maintain a wide foot-base while on the run.

2. Before contact, drop your hips (not your head) to achieve an up-climbing spring from your legs and back.

3. "Bull" your neck for stability and safety.

4. Aim your headgear on a course through the defender's inside armpit and drive him to the outside. If he charges inside, or if you find a linebacker at an inside disadvantage, you may elect to cut off his outside to allow the runner to slide off your block.

5. Establish shoulder contact close within the "V" of your neck and shoulder, forcefully snapping both forearms upward.

6. Drive your opponent from an up-climb with continuous steps, blinding his vision and depriving him of solid traction.

7. During your up-climb, rotate your hips into the cut-off area with wide, choppy steps to attain a cut-off advantage! (See Diagram 4-15).

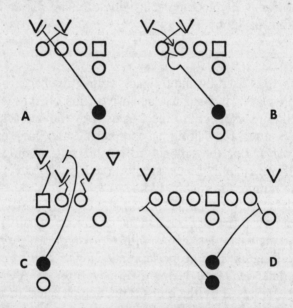

Diagram 4-15

Turn-In Block:

Used by a blocking back as he turns the corner and confronts a soft-playing secondary defender. The blocking back should throw his block only when close enough to make inside shoulder-contact while on the run. The blocker's momentum should be kept upfield as he seals off the outside running lane with his body (See Diagram 4-16).

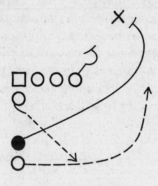

Diagram 4-16

Sideline Block:

Used by a blocking back when he approaches the corner and confronts a secondary defender advancing toward the scrimmage line to contain a wide run. As the challenging opponent is met at the corner, the blocker should attempt to knock him into the sideline, making contact with his bottomside shoulder. As contact is made, the blocker's hips should maintain a near-parallel position with the sideline for cut-off purposes. A sustained follow-through is important in preventing a defensive recovery (See Diagram 4-17).

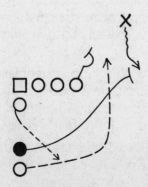

Diagram 4-17

POP AND PIVOT PASS PROTECTION

There are several theories and methods of protecting the quarterback in his pass pocket. Since the Slot-I concentrates heavily on a pull-up and play-action pass release behind the tackle, with agressive onside blocking, the big concern lies in protecting the passer's blind side. A backside cup protection is necessary, and its blocking technique must be consistent with standard blocking procedures. Opinions differ as to how a pass protection cup should be formed, but one point has universal agreement: the inside gaps must be closed! The following is a method that protects the inside without giving a premature tip-off of a pass play call.

APPLICATION

Stance:

1. Take the prescribed 3-point stance with a wide, parallel foot-base as used with the shoulder and scramble blocks.
2. Place slight pressure on your grounded hand, without leaning backward or pointing in either direction.

Uncoil and Recovery:

1. Explode outward and "pop" your assigned opponent with a high chest block into his jersey numbers to break his charge. If you do not have a defensive lineman aligned over you or if an obvious passing situation exists, take a check-skip inside. However, try to false-key opposing linebackers.
2. If an initial contact is made, recover by *pivoting* on your *inside foot*, keep a semi-crouched stance, and *squeeze* your tail to the middle with shuffling steps. (Refer to Diagram 4-18)
3. Assume a zone-blocking assignment, awaiting the first rusher to appear from inside-out. If an uncovered blocker has no inside penetration to appear, he proceeds to pedal backwards and pick up the on-charging defensive end.
4. Line up your head and tail between the innermost pass rusher and the pull-up point of the quarterback in his pass pocket.

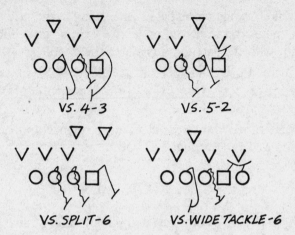

Diagram 4-18 Examples of Backside Pass-Protection (assignment covered in Chapter 5)

5. As the opponent charges into the protection cup, explode again and pop him abruptly into his jersey numbers with a high chest block.

6. Recoil and shuffle backward, assuming a new hitting position. Try to barricade the pass-rush lane that leads to the junction point of the pass pocket triangle.

Follow-Through:

1. Finally, cut the challenger down with an explosive scramble, keeping the opponent to the outside.

2. If you sense the football in flight, release immediately and cover upfield. Your presence upfield can give blocking assistance to your team's pass receiver or prevent a run-back if an interception occurs.

Tips and Summation:

1. Apply all the fundamental techniques of a shoulder block in regard to stance, hitting position and follow-through.

2. When assuming a semi-crouch recoil, keep your head up and tail low.

3. Keep the inside gap protected, allowing no inside daylight. Detect and squeeze-off line slants and linebacker loops.

4. Make the oncoming pass rusher take the initiative. Don't be anxious and leave the protective cup, or be influenced into an awkward position that leaves the middle area vulnerable.

5. Cover the passed football upfield, to give blocking interference for the runner and to protect against an interception.

6. Remember your pass-blocking sequence: pop and pivot, pop and recover, cut and cover.

CLOSING COMMENTS

Daily exposure to blocking assignments and correct procedure is a simple, but effective means of developing positive attitudes, sound technique and crisp execution. To teach blocking fundamentals properly, use body-length dummies, blocking sleds and small-group contact drills. To teach quickness effectively, review the team take-off drills daily and emphasize them with stop-watch timing. From the instructional viewpoint, always try to use a pragmatic approach: use only practical and functional drills that relate to scrimmage situations.

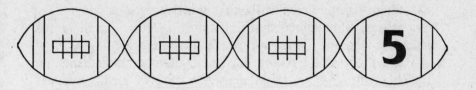

FORMULATING BLOCKING RULES AND PATTERNS FOR THE SLOT-I

The one phase of football that never can be overtaught is blocking assignments! Multiple blocking schemes are commonplace in modern offensive football and are the very foundation of the resourceful Slot-I. A variable blocking approach can give your offense a distinct advantage in forcing a defense to respond to the many ways it can be blocked. A flexible blocking system gives the defense more to worry about than the mere snap count and play flow—it must react to different blocking angles, power combinations and option intimidations.

But flexibility can be taken to an extreme. Confusion must be avoided at all costs. Each lineman should have a mental picture of a play's overall blocking scheme, so that he can carry out his assignment automatically. Then, an adjustment to a changed defensive situation can be readily made. It is vital to winning that defensive pursuit be adequately slowed, that linebackers are blocked aggressively and that no one is left unblocked or is allowed to penetrate the line.

The solution to the paradox of simplicity with flexibility, is in teaching your football players to:

(1) Block defensive alignments by recognition, using the "base rule" as a guiding reference.

(2) Emphasize blocking patterns, not rhetoric and memorization.

A base rule covers area identification in straight blocking situations. Using a base (area) rule identification of defensive assignments is more reliable than a numbering system when facing various stack alignments, shuffling multiple fronts, and individual defenders who are aligned at a poor cut-off blocking angle.

The process of teaching linemen their base assignments and blocking patterns against set defenses is that of "logical sequence." This means that blocking application is taught step by step, against all current defenses, through *constant repetition*. Time spent on visual application is time spent wisely. By teaching recognition of defensive fronts to offensive linemen, all base and pattern assignments can be carried out without hesitation or fault. Learning to achieve proper cut-off position must be a part of your instructional process.

Base assignments and pattern blocking can be taught in the same way as a pass receiver is taught—*by association with a descriptive play name*. For example, a blocking pattern such as the 3- or 4-hole Cross Trap, a play which involves a cross-buck action in the backfield with a trap block at the attack area, is taught through *repetition* against familiar defensive alignments. Its descriptive name aids in relating a special blocking pattern to the play-side linemen.

A practical drill for teaching all play assignments is the "Blocking Pattern Drill." Through this drill, linemen can be exposed to various alignments while necessary techniques and skills can be emphasized and executed. You can set up any combination of line positions: center and guards—center, guards and tackles—half a line—or a complete line. This invaluable drill concept can serve three functional uses:

(1) Form and assignments can be taught by stepping through each player's responsibility.

(2) Technique, timing and assignments can be taught at full speed against dummies.

(3) Execution and assignments can be taught in live contact through a simulation of full-speed scrimmage (no backfield). (Diagram 5-1 A, B, C, and D)

In the process of teaching assignments and skills with this drill, a coach should start with just a few plays within a single series. The basic keystone offense should be learned first, then the extras can be added later.

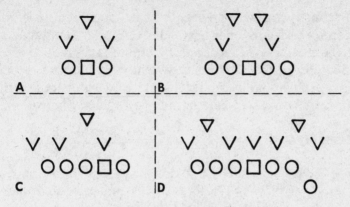

Diagram 5-1 Blocking Pattern Drill

GUIDELINES FOR BASE BLOCKING

The Slot-I can make use of straight plays with base blocking that is equal to, if not better than, other comparable systems. Base blocking refers to solid one-on-one blocking at the line of scrimmage.

In a majority of cases, base blocking is used at the backside of a running play. To the play-side, either base blocking, pattern blocking or a combination of the two can be used. Thus, a play call will usually consist of the play-hole number, plus a descriptive name that relates a base block or pattern block at the point of attack.

The Base-blocking rule has three areas of recognition:

(1) Inside

(2) Over

(3) Outside

Explanation:

(1) If a defender is aligned to your *inside*, block him!

(2) If no one is there (N/T), block the defender aligned directly *over* you.

(3) N/T, block the nearest defender aligned to your *outside*.

For instructional reference, the base-blocking rule is broken down into "backside" and "play-side" categories. This gives a line coach the exactness that is necessary for him to cover all foreseeable situations. Even if a numbering system were substituted for rule blocking, similar problem areas would exist, as identified in the following section, and would have to be handled comparably.

Application

Backside Tackle: Base rule. All middle plays, sustain block; away plays, block for 3 counts and cover acrossfield over the play-hole area.

Special Instructions—

(1) If a defensive tackle is pinching inside, sustain the block.

(2) If the middle is outnumbered, use the "inside" rule (loop block the front lineman of a stack or Split-4, angling from underneath).

Backside Guard: Base rule. Block for 4 counts and release toward play-hole area (block and cover).

Special Instructions—

(1) In applying the base rule, seek out the first lineman or linebacker on the *inside of center*. Loop block a stack or Split-4, cutting off the linebacker from pursuit.

Center: Base rule with the following modifications:

(1) Read the "inside" rule as a play-side gap. Against a Split-4 or Stack-4 look, block the *play-side linebacker* as implied by the "inside" rule.

(2) N/T, use "over" rule.

(3) N/T, block backside linebacker *after* checking for a play-side gap penetration.

Play-side Guard: Base rule.

Play-side Tackle: Base rule. Exception: block "outside" vs. a Split-4 front on middle base assignments.

Tight End: (Play-side)

(1) Apply the base rule to an onside Cross Trap, Isolate or Sweep play.

(2) A "Force" assignment is given for straight plays in the interior, which do not involve the tight end as a blocker on the line. Release outside the defensive end, and take the outside pass defender on a deep route; then break down, maintain a wide foot-base, stalk the opponent, and block. Observe pass-coverage breakdowns.

Special Instructions—

(1) If covered by an outside linebacker (5-3 defense, etc.), bump the opponent for a count before releasing into the outside perimeter.

(Backside)

(1) Penetrate the middle crease and block the nearest pass defender! Release inside the defensive end, to make a slide into the deep middle.

(2) Block the near safety on inside trap plays (do not allow the safety to play the role of linebacker when he recognizes a trap-blocking pattern—give your ball carrier a running funnel up the deep middle).

Slot Back (Play-side)

(1) Apply the base rule to an onside Cross Trap, Isolate or Sweep plays.

(2) A "Force" assignment is given for straight plays in the interior that do not involve the slot back as a blocker. Release outside the defensive end, and take the nearside safety (#2 from the outside) on a deep route; then break-down, maintain a wide foot-base, stalk the opponent and block. Observe pass-coverage breakdowns.

Special Instructions—

(1) If facing a "loaded" defense (Split-4, Wide-Tackle 6, etc.), take a wide split to remove the outside linebacker from his

inside support role and into a wider pass-coverage commitment. Then "force" him upfield on inside plays and options. Note: remember to align in normal position on the Tackle Trap and Isolate Option plays.

(Backside)

(1) Penetrate the middle crease and block the nearside safety (#2 from the outside). Release inside the defensive end, if not congested. If the secondary has rotated, seek out the free safety.

Split End: (Play-side)

(1) Force! Take the outside pass defender on a deep route; then break down, maintain a wide foot-base, stalk the opponent and block.

Special Assignments—

(1) On off-tackle, keeper and lead-back option plays to the onside, use a shield block against any walk-away linebacker, rover back or inverted safety. If N/T, seek out the deep safety.

(Backside)

(1) Penetrate the middle crease (between the #1 and #2 secondary defenders) and block the nearest pass defender. Try to take two opponents upfield, removing them from run support.

Fullback & Tailback: Clean-up block any stray defender after carrying out decoy-play fakes on sequence plays such as the Cross Trap, Base Option and Isolate Keep or Option.

TEACHING BLOCKING PATTERNS

If a soundly-coached defensive team could be whipped with base blocking alone, it would be unnecessary to use multiple blocking patterns. But, unfortunately for the offense, this is not the case. A good defensive ball club must be attacked in a *variety* of ways. To move the football upfield with consistency, the offense must give the defense problems that can stalemate its strongest personnel.

The concept of blocking patterns broadens the Slot-I into a comprehensive offense. In most instances, a blocking pattern involves onside linemen at the point of attack, but may include a backside pulling guard or tackle.

For simplicity, blocking patterns are taught by descriptive names, *not* by play-hole numbers. Pattern blocking, as such, is specialized and should be taught in specialized terms.

Application

PATTERN:	SPECIALIZED ASSIGNMENTS:
Quick Trap (FB)	Backside tackle—fill for the pulling guard; if not applicable (N/A), block base. Backside guard—pull from the line behind the center and trap the first defender to appear (lineman or linebacker) in the play-side center-guard hole. Center—block backside; if N/T, block base (5-3). Play-side guard—block inside; if gapped, or if the opponent is the target of a trap, block outside. Play-side tackle—block base; if Split-4(6), block the outside defender. Tight end—block the near safety when aligned at play-side.
Tackle Trap (SB)	Backside tackle—pull from the line behind the center, and trap the first defender to penetrate. Backside guard—block base. Center—block over; if N/T, block backside. Play-side guard—block inside; if the opponent is the target of a trap, block outside. Play-side tackle—block the near linebacker; if N/A, block outside. Play-side tight end—block the near safety.
Draw (middle-TB)	Interior linemen—use pass protection blocks, hooking each defender away from the tight guard area. If covered by a linebacker, protect the inside rush lane against a blitz or line slant for 2 full counts. If the inside lane is clear, then go after the assigned linebacker within the short-pass coverage zone.

Isolate (TB)	Play-side linemen—overlook the inside linebacker within the attack area, then apply the base-blocking rule (a double-team block often will occur inside the isolation point). Play-side tight end or slot back—block over or outside, turning the opponent outward.
Isolate Keep (QB) -or-Option (QB-SB)	Playside linemen—use the same blocking guideline as with the Isolate play: overlook the inside linebacker within the attack area, and apply the base-blocking rule. On the option, the tight end slams his opponent, the defensive end, for 1 full count, then releases outside to force (and block) the defensive halfback. On the Keep, the slot back and split end adjust into a wide (flex) slot to improve blocking angles, then use their respective cut and shield blocks.
Cross Trap (TB)	Backside guard—pull from the line behind the center and trap the first defender outside the offensive tackle. Center—block backside; N/T, block base (5-3). Play-side guard—block inside (may fold block on the linebacker vs. a Split-4 or 6 defense). Play-side tackle—block inside; if N/A, or if opponent is the target of a trap, block outside. Tight end or slot back at play-side—apply the base rule.
Trap (off tackle- FB)	Tackle and tight end or slot back at play-side—block inside. Play-side guard—pull from the line and trap block the onside defensive end.
Lead Option (QB-TB)	Interior linemen at play-side—base rule. Play-side tackle—block inside if the linebacker is over (4-3, etc). Tight end or slot back at play-side—block inside; if N/T, block over (slot back should flex vs. a Split-4 or 5-3 defense).

Power (TB)	Tackle and tight end or slot back at play-side—block inside. Play-side guard—block base, unless the linebacker is over; then block inside.
Sweep (TB)	Backside guard—pull from the line behind the center and lead interference around the corner. Backside tackle—fill for the pulling guard. Interior linemen at play-side—apply the base rule. Tight end at play-side—reach and hook. Slot back and split end at play-side—adjust into a flex alignment and then use respective cut and shield blocks.
Waggle (QB bootleg)	Backside (slot) guard—pull behind the center and lead block at the defensive end's outside number. Backside (Tight Side) linemen—use pop and pivot protection.
Screen Middle (TB)	Interior linemen—apply the base rule and use a convincing bump block, allowing each defender to fight through. Then release 3 yards beyond the line of scrimmage with the center forming the apex of a tight-knit wedge. The human wall of blockers moves forward as "Ball" is yelled by the runner.
Screen R-L (TB)	Play-side tackle—block base for 3 counts, slide 7 yards toward the sideline, set up a screen-pass wall and take the outside responsibility. Play-side guard—block base for 3 counts, slide to link the wall from inside and take responsibility for the area inside the teammate. Center—block base for 3 full counts, slide and curl back to pick up the backside drift; then follow-up into the wall on the runner's signal, taking care not to clip. The blocking wall must release together in front of the runner as the ball is thrown, then head up the sideline as "Ball" is yelled by the runner.

Innovations

Fullback Lead-Block	Used as an alternative to an isolation play. One-on-one (base) blocking is used with the fullback assigned to lead through the play-side guard-tackle hole and pick up any loose floaters that may be choking-off the attack area.
"X" and "Y" Blocks	Used as a blocking change-up on straight hand-offs and cross bucks. With "X" blocking, the play-side guard and tackle exchange defensive opponents by cross blocking—with the outside blocker (tackle) firing across first. With "Y" blocking, the inside blocker (guard) fires across first, which is a useful tactic with a cross-action play.
Off-Tackle Slant Block	Used as a blocking pattern change-up on off-tackle slants. Play-side base blocking is used with the exception of the on-side tight end or slot back who block inside. The fullback is responsible for blocking the defensive end as the backside guard pulls from the line and leads through the attack hole. This pattern can complement a talented runner who has an eye for soft spots along the scrimmage line.
Fold Block	Used against off-set stacks as found internally in a Split-4 defense. The play-side tackle and guard exchange blocking assignments in similarity to a cross block. The tackle steps first, as the guard steps around and goes upward to pick up the inside linebacker. Its purpose is to attain an improved blocking angle on a stack alignment.
Wedge Block	May be used with short-yardage sneaks and straight hand-offs. All interior linemen pinch inside immediately on the ball snap, lock shoulder pads, and continue with short,

driving steps to create forceful momentum. The idea is to raise the defending linemen up, deprive them of traction and force a backward retreat.

PASS BLOCKING GUIDELINES FOR INTERIOR LINEMEN

Play-side Tackle	Base rule (pop and pivot block, aggressively). If covered by a linebacker, check blitz and then block the *closest* defensive lineman to appear.
Play-side Guard	Base rule (pop and pivot block, aggressively). If covered by a linebacker, check blitz and then block inside on the nose guard.
Center	Base rule (get cut-off position). If covered by a linebacker, check for a blitz or inside slant. If N/T, cup block behind the line of scrimmage and seek out the defensive end.
Backside Guard	Cup protection (pop and pivot). If covered by a linebacker, check for a blitz and then drop backward to pick up the defensive end.
Backside Tackle	The same guidelines apply as for the backside guard.

ILLUSTRATIVE ASSIGNMENT CHARTS AND DIAGRAMS

In tying together all loose ends, the blocking assignments for the keystone attack shall be charted by play category, then diagramed against the most common defensive alignments. Since all defenses have their strong points, not all plays are necessarily ideal against each defensive alignment. Notice should be taken, however, that many overload defensive fronts are at a serious disadvantage in effectively covering a slot back and split end combination.

Table 5-1

TYPE PLAY	BACKSIDE END	BACKSIDE TACKLE	BACKSIDE GUARD	CENTER	PLAY-SIDE GUARD	PLAY-SIDE TACKLE	PLAY-SIDE RECEIVERS
1-2 Base and 1-2 Base Option	Crease	Base (sustain block on hand-off; release on option). Loop a Split-4(6) stack	Base	Base (vs. Split-4(6), block onside LB); N/T, backside LB (standard guideline)	Base	Base; block outside vs. a Split-4(6) on hand-off	Force: TE blocks inside vs. a loaded 8-man front
1-2 (3-4) Isolate	Crease	Base; Split-4(6), block outside	Base; Split-4(6), block the down lineman	Over; N/T, backside LB	Ignore LB, apply base rule	Ignore LB, apply base rule (block outside vs. Split-4(6)	TE or SB-block over or outside (turn opponent outward) SE-force
1-2 (3-4) Isolate Keep-or-Option	Crease	(above)	(above)	(above)	(above)	(above)	OPTION: TE blocks DE 1 count, then force KEEP: SB-cut block. SE-shield block

Play							
1-2 Quick Trap	Crease	Fill for pulling guard; if N/A, apply base rule	Pull behind center and trap first defender to appear in C-G hole	Block backside; N/T, block base (5-3)	Inside; unless opponent is trap target, block outside	Base; Split-4(6), block outside	SB & SE-force TE-block the near safety
21-22 Tackle Trap	Crease	Pull behind center and trap first defender to penetrate	Base	Over; N/T, block backside	Inside; unless opponent is trap target, block outside	Block near LB; if N/A, block outside	TE-block across-field on the near safety
1-2 Draw	SE-post route	Interior linemen use aggressive pass-protection blocks. Defensive linemen must be hooked away from the tight guard area. If covered by a LB, protect inside rush lane for 2 counts, then go after LB in his coverage zone.					TE-block across-field on the near safety
3-4 Cross Trap	Crease	Base, 3 counts and release. Loop a Split-4(6)	Pull behind center and trap first defender outside offensive tackle	Block backside; N/T, block base (5-3)	Inside (may fold block LB on a Split-4(6)	Inside; if N/A, or if opponent is trap target, block outside	TE or SB-block base. SE-force

Table 5-2

TYPE PLAY	BACKSIDE END	BACKSIDE TACKLE	BACKSIDE GUARD	CENTER	PLAY-SIDE GUARD	PLAY-SIDE TACKLE	PLAY-SIDE RECEIVERS
5-6 Trap	Crease	Base, 3 counts and release. Loop a Split-4(6)	Base	Base (check play-side gap)	Pull and trap on-side DE	Inside; N/T, block over	TE or SB-inside; N/T, block over. SE-shield block.
5-6 Power	Crease	Base, 3 counts and release. Loop a Split-4(6)	Base	Base	Base; unless LB is "over," block inside	Inside; N/T, block over	TE or SB-inside; N/T, block over. SE-shield block.
15-16 Lead Option	Crease	Base, 3 counts and release. Loop a Split-4(6)	Base	Base	Base	Base; unless LB "over," then block inside if applicable	TE or SB-inside; N/T, block over, SE-shield block.
7-8 Sweep	Crease	Fill for pulling guard. Loop a Split-4(6)	Pull and lead play around corner	Base (check backside gap)	Base	Base	TE-reach and hook. ——— SB-cut block. SE-shield block.

Waggle (run-pass)	Crease	Pop and pivot (squeeze-off inside)	Pull behind center and lead block at DE's outside	Base (pop and pivot)	Base; LB "over"-check blitz and then block inside	Base; LB "over"-check blitz and then block closest lineman	TE-in and out route
Screen Middle	TE-go route, then stalk and seal off inside	Bump block and release; merge into developing wedge of screen wall		Bump block and release-form apex of wedge 3 yds. deep	Bump block and release; merge into developing wedge of screen wall		SE-go route. SB-post route (block near safety).
Screen Right or Left	Assigned route	Pop and pivot	Pop and pivot	Base, 3 counts-slide and cover backside drift; follow-up	Base, 3 counts-slide and help form screen wall	Base, 3 counts-slide 7 yds. and set up the screen wall	Assigned route

Table 5-3

PLAY CATEGORY	5-2 UMBRELLA
1-2 BASE & BASE OPTION	
1-2 (3-4) ISOLATE	
1-2 (3-4) ISOLATE KEEP	
1-2 QUICK TRAP	
21-22 TACKLE TRAP	
1-2 DRAW	
3-4 CROSS TRAP	

Table 5-3 Continued

PLAY CATEGORY	4-3 INVERT
1-2 BASE & BASE OPTION	
1-2 (3-4) ISOLATE	
1-2 (3-4) ISOLATE KEEP	
1-2 QUICK TRAP	
21-22 TACKLE TRAP	
1-2 DRAW	
3-4 CROSS TRAP	

Table 5-3 Continued

PLAY CATEGORY	SPLIT-4
1-2 BASE & BASE OPTION	(OPTION BEST TO SLOT SIDE)
1-2 (3-4) ISOLATE	
1-2 (3-4) ISOLATE KEEP	
1-2 QUICK TRAP	
21-22 TACKLE TRAP	
1-2 DRAW	
3-4 CROSS TRAP	

Table 5-4

PLAY CATEGORY	5-2 UMBRELLA
5-6 TRAP	
5-6 POWER	
15-16 LEAD OPTION	
7-8 SWEEP	
15-16 PASS PROTECTION	
WAGGLE PASS PROTECTION	
BACK-PEDAL PROTECTION (SUPPLEMENT)	

Table 5-4 Continued

PLAY CATEGORY	4 - 3 INVERT
5-6 TRAP	
5-6 POWER	
15-16 LEAD OPTION	
7-8 SWEEP	
15-16 PASS PROTECTION	
WAGGLE PASS PROTECTION	
BACK-PEDAL PROTECTION (SUPPLEMENT)	

Table 5-4 Continued

PLAY CATEGORY	SPLIT-4
5-6 TRAP	 *(REDUCE LB'S W/SLOT SIDE OVERLOAD)*
5-6 POWER	 FOLD BLOCK (4-HOLE)
15-16 LEAD OPTION	 FOLD BLOCK · SWITCH BLOCK
7-8 SWEEP	
15-16 PASS PROTECTION	
WAGGLE PASS PROTECTION	
BACK-PEDAL PROTECTION (SUPPLEMENT)	

Table 5-5

PLAY CATEGORY	WIDE-T 6-2
1-2 BASE & BASE OPTION	
1-2 (3-4) ISOLATE	
1-2 (3-4) ISOLATE OPTION	
1-2 QUICK TRAP	
21-22 TACKLE TRAP	
1-2 DRAW	
3-4 CROSS TRAP	

Table 5-5 Continued

PLAY CATEGORY	GAP-7 (8)
1-2 BASE & BASE OPTION	
1-2 (3-4) ISOLATE	
1-2 (3-4) ISOLATE OPTION	
1-2 QUICK TRAP	
21-22 TACKLE TRAP	
1-2 DRAW	
3-4 CROSS TRAP	

Table 5-5 Continued

PLAY CATEGORY	5-3 EAGLE
1-2 BASE & BASE OPTION	
1-2 (3-4) ISOLATE	
1-2 (3-4) ISOLATE OPTION	
1-2 QUICK TRAP	
21-22 TACKLE TRAP	
1-2 DRAW	
3-4 CROSS TRAP	

Table 5-6

PLAY CATEGORY	WIDE-T 6-2
5-6 TRAP	
5-6 POWER	
15-16 LEAD OPTION	
7-8 SWEEP	
15-16 PASS PROTECTION	
WAGGLE PASS PROTECTION	
BACK-PEDAL PROTECTION (SUPPLEMENT)	

Table 5-6 Continued

PLAY CATEGORY	GAP-7 (8)
5-6 TRAP	
5-6 POWER	
15-16 LEAD OPTION	
7-8 SWEEP	
15-16 PASS PROTECTION	
WAGGLE PASS PROTECTION	
BACK-PEDAL PROTECTION (SUPPLEMENT)	

Table 5-6 Continued

PLAY CATEGORY	5-3 EAGLE
5-6 TRAP	
5-6 POWER	
15-16 LEAD OPTION	
7-8 SWEEP	
15-16 PASS PROTECTION	
WAGGLE PASS PROTECTION	
BACK-PEDAL PROTECTION (SUPPLEMENT)	

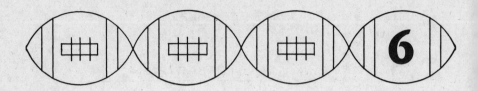

PUTTING THE SLOT-I INTO OPERATION

The Slot-I offense is an attack of many specialties. Not unlike other offensive systems, it is important to give your Slot-I offense adequate player-orientation in formation structure, hole numbering, play terminology, huddle system, cadence, play automatics, hole spacings and offensive development. Unless this foundation is given proper attention, it would be foolish to assume that a successful attack could be launched against an organized defense. To throw an unprepared offense into the waiting hands of a hungry defense in pre-season practice is a sure way to destroy offensive confidence. Without the benefit of technique and timing, a premature scrimmage against a defense with equal personnel is like asking for sheer disaster, especially if the defensive team is given freedom to slant and blitz.

To develop confidence, we always use breakdown offensive drills to work on play assignments and the isolated parts of our running and passing offense, before venturing into a full-scale scrimmage. Also, we refrain from re-introducing our defensive gaming during early spring drills, thereby refining our defensive reading techniques and pursuit reaction, while striving to jell our offense.

STRUCTURE OF THE FLIP-FLOP

A rebirth of the flop-over principle for offensive linemen has had a tremendous impact on modern football. As stressed in Chapter 3, a flip-flop line gives the Slot-I offense a strategic potential that is comparable to the blocking power of the old, unbalanced-line Single Wing formation.

The right and left formations are flip-flopped, so that there can be both a constant slot side and tight side. For those who tend to be "right-handed" in calling formations, a "Slot Right" call would not work to a disadvantage. The stronger blockers would then be located to the offensive left, opposite the "running-side" of the defense.

The hole numbering of a Slot-I can remain stationary, so the numbers need not change when a flop-over occurs. Since much of our offense is mirrored, we do not switch our hole numbers. All even numbers, therefore, are always on the right side, and the odd numbers are found on the left side. The smaller hole numbers are located in the middle, with the count becoming larger as the numbers go outward (See Diagrams 6-1 and 6-2).

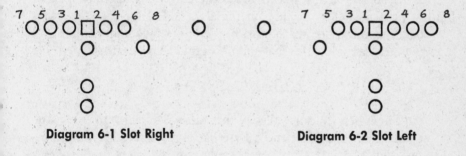

Diagram 6-1 Slot Right   Diagram 6-2 Slot Left

PLAY NAMING

We call plays by a single-digit *hole number,* followed by the play *name*. This eliminates quarterback error in calling a wrong running-back number when making a play selection under pressure. Since adopting this method a few years ago, broken plays have become almost extinct. To illustrate the simplicity of a single-digit play call, a fullback-trap play to the left side of center would be verbalized as "1 Quick Trap" which indicates first that the 1-hole is to be run, and second shows the type of play (a dive-action trap to the fullback) that will hit the play hole.

The quarterback and slot back are the only backfield members that have a play number. The quarterback's assigned number is "1" and the slot back's assigned number is "2"—the fullback and tailback do not have assigned numbers. When either the quarterback or slot back becomes a designated runner, a double-digit play number is used for clarity ("16 Lead Option"; "21 Tackle Trap").

Our passes are called by the *pocket number* on all pull-up passes, followed by the pass pattern ("16 Pass, Fan": "15 Pass, Divide"). Play-action passes, from a tailback fake of the off-tackle Power play or fullback fake of the middle Base play, are thrown from the same slot side pocket but are indicated by *play name*, followed by the word "Pass" and then the pass pattern ("5 Power Pass, X"; "2 Base Pass, Cross"). Supplemental sprint-out calls are designated as "18 (or 17) Pass," followed by the name of the pass pattern ("18 Pass, See-Saw"; "17 Pass, Scissor"). A centralized pass pocket is designated as "Back-Pedal Pass," which is followed by the name of the pattern.

A bootleg-action pass is called exclusively by *direction* because the pass pocket is formed on the tight side, opposite the usual pocket, and the slot guard must be alerted to pull from the line and block the far side defensive end ("Waggle Pass, Left").

HUDDLE SYSTEM

The open huddle allows the offensive team to view the opposing defense while the quarterback announces his play selection. Any huddle system is applicable, but the open huddle allows the quarterback, with his back to the defense, to be free from some of the distractions that could hinder his concentration.

Prior to the gathering of the huddle, the center commands "Down!" to his front ranks to get the huddle organized with the interior linemen assuming a hands-on-knees position. Before the quarterback steps up to the huddle, he automatically looks at the yard-line chains, the down marker and the yard-line marker, *before* calling any plays.

A play is called in the huddle in the following sequence: (1) formation, (2) play selection and snap count to his right in the huddle, (3) pause and excuse the center to get a preliminary pre-snap position over the ball, and (4) repeat the play and snap count to his left in the huddle. The quarterback breaks the huddle into formation by commanding "Break!" If a line flop-over is necessary, the slot side goes first (to the left), and the tight side—after a delay—goes second, to the right (See Diagram 6-3).

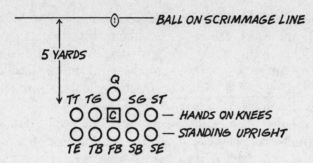

Diagram 6-3 Huddle System

CADENCE

The best cadence in football is a combination of broken and rhythmic counts. After trying several systems in the past, we have settled upon a simple "Down" command, followed by a live or dead automatic, and concluded with a rhythmic count of "Set-Hike." The ball snap can be called on "Down," on a dead automatic number, or on "Set," which are all non-rhythm, or on "Hike," which is in rhythm with "Set." This gives four opportunities in our cadence to snap the football with a minimal chance of mistakes.

When a ball snap is called on "Hike," the rhythm method has helped our offensive line to anticipate their exploding charge from the scrimmage line without jumping off-sides. Straight, non-rhythm methods that have been tried previously gave us many problems, which resulted in the use of a quick count on the first sound most of the time. This, no doubt, was favorable to the defensive opponent. To ensure that the squad's reflex action is timed at the end of the cadence, we place our snap-out emphasis on "Hike" during spring drills.

SEMI-AUTOMATICS: A SIMPLE SAFEGUARD

Many coaches avoid play changes at the line of scrimmage because of the increased possibility of error by any one of the eleven offensive players. Not only is there the problem that the quarterback might not make a wise choice from among his many play selections because of the emotional stress of competition, but also all the offensive players must interpret the play switch, then mentally change the original play assignment before the snap of the football.

With these problems in mind, a different approach has been adopted, one which can be used without disturbing our play-call system. This system, as explained, designates a hole number, plus a descriptive name. After evaluating several current methods, a "semi-automatic" system was devised for making a play-call while on the scrimmage line.

When the quarterback wishes to use a semi-automatic, he predetermines his play type while in the huddle—one which can be mirrored to either side of the line—and then selects his play-hole at the line of scrimmage. In his huddle call, the word "automatic" is substituted for the play-hole number, then the play name is announced. After the huddle breaks into formation at the line of scrimmage, the quarterback calls "Down"; next, he calls the live hole number, then he commands the ball snap, which is preset on "Set." For example, if "Automatic Quick Trap" were called in the huddle, the quarterback would designate either "Two" or "One" on the scrimmage line, which would result in a quick-hitting fullback trap-play, to the right or left of center, on the snap count of "Set."

A semi-automatic system is ideal for high school and can be easily installed. This system is good especially when there is uncertainty about a defensive shift. It has proven itself to be mistake-free, simple to use and effective in coming through successfully in tough-yardage situations. It is advisable, however, to avoid an overexposure of semi-automatics during a game, and to always use a dead number in normal cadence.

HOLE SPACING

Variable hole spacings can increase the probability of offensive success when their use is applied intelligently. There are some offensive systems, such as the pure Split-T and Veer-T, that require an exact adherence to rigid line spacings in order to spread the defense and explore their highly-disciplined option series. "Pro" oriented offensive systems, in contrast, are often flexible so that blocking angles can be exploited.

In the Slot-I plan of attack, *standard* line spacing should be taught first. *Variable* adjustments should be taught after the squad fully understands the philosophical makeup of the offense. When variable spacing is used, its objectives should be (1) to tighten or spread the defense and, (2) to gain improved blocking angles within a blocking pattern. The interior defense should be spread at the point of attack for most of the straight-ahead running game, since it is unwise to choke off the inside plays with overly-conservative line splits. To achieve proper trap-blocking angles, however, the linemen that block inside should be tightened somewhat to assure crisp execution. End runs and predetermined pitch-out plays would normally necessitate minimum splits, with an exception taken when a desirable inside blocking angle can be gained by taking a wider split.

If a veer (triple) option is included in the attack, it is essential to use preset line spacings. This is because of the critical timing factor involved in the hand-off exchange, and in the need to spread out the defenders who must be read on the option. Standard spacing should be used for the veer option from an "I" backfield, but maximum spacing is recommended for a Slot-Veer alignment (See Diagram 6-4 and 6-5 for line-spacing illustrations).

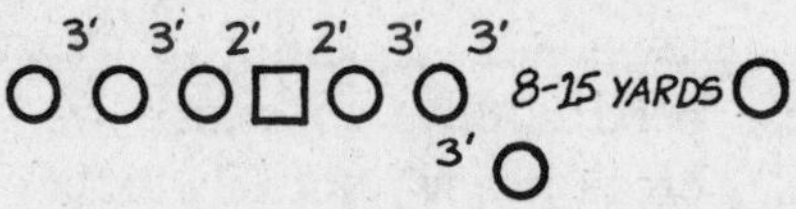

```
    3'  3'  2'  2'  3'  3'
    O   O   O   □   O   O   8-15 YARDS  O
                    3'
                    O
```

Diagram 6-4 Standard Spacings

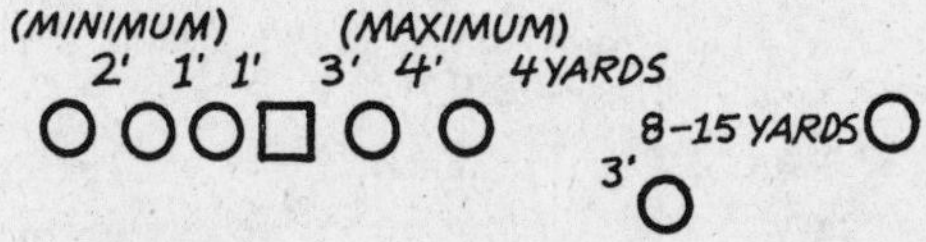

```
   (MINIMUM)      (MAXIMUM)
   2'  1'  1'    3'  4'   4 YARDS
   O   O O   □   O   O        8-15 YARDS  O
                          3'
                          O
```

Diagram 6-5 Variable Adjustments

PRACTICE ORGANIZATION

For developmental purposes, the components of football can be broken down into three separate phases—individual, unit and team. All three of these phases, therefore, should be given consideration when planning a composite practice schedule. To ensure a progression of learning experiences, there must be adequate repetition of the basic fundamentals, plus a planned overlap of team review. To guarantee efficiency in planning, we use various master schedules for spring, pre-season and fall training, with time-blocks (training periods) set aside for all the vital areas of football, including offense, defense and the kicking game. With properly sequenced time-block practice schedules, staff members can select the drills they wish to use each day which meet the needs of their assigned group at every stage of the season. A time-block schedule also assures consistency and concentrated emphasis upon each phase of the game, yet allows for flexibility in training and teaching methods. With copying-machine time-block sheets made readily available for the staff, a head coach's planning time can be shortened because of the organization designed into the master schedules. Economy in planning time is helpful, especially in situations where the coaching staff has a full, classroom teaching load.

With a time-block concept, nothing of importance is overlooked, and specific areas of unit work involving isolated groups can receive their necessary training time. The Slot-I's passing attack and blocking patterns are always given faithful attention during the time-block allotted to breakdown work with the offensive units.

Since our time-block periods are preset for all the phases of football, continuity is maintained and we are least likely to lose sight of our long-term objectives and goals. In theory, an educational concept has been applied in which we take the game of football as a whole, break it down into its functional parts through unit drills, and then put the game back together again for rehearsal and polishing through team drills (See Diagrams 6-6 through 6-11).

Diagram 6-6

PRE-SEASON PRACTICE
SCHEDULE

August and Spring Drills

Time (Min) Time-Block

_____ (15) *Warmup Period* (Calesthenics; knee & groin isometrics; stretching; agility & reaction; quick starts; tires).

_____ (10) *Backfield Specialty:* (Select) Climb blocking drills; option drills; play rehearsal; other _____.

Linemen Specialty: (Select) Sled explosions; sled blocking drills; sled agility drills; other _.

_____ (20) *Pass Pattern Breakdown:* (Select) Warmup drills; single receiver routes; skeleton patterns; other _____. (TE's alternate below)

Diagram 6-6 Continued

Line Blocking Breakdown: (Select) Board drills; 2-on-2 with runner; 3-on-3 with runner & free LB; blocking pattern drill; pass protection drill; other _____.

____ (20) *Secondary Breakdown:* (Select) Technique & reaction drills; 1-vs-1 dog-fight coverage; lock-up & release tackling drills; perimeter drill vs live patterns (award winner points); other __. (LB's alternate below).

Defensive Line & LB Breakdown: (Select) Pursuit recognition & reaction; pass rush with LB coverage; fumble recovery drills; read & destroy technique; sweep containing drills; LB fill & scrape; tackling drills; middle defense drill; outside defense drill; stunt technique & rehearsal; scout report; other _____.

____ (5) Water break.

____ (20) *Team Defense.*

____ (20) *Team Offense.*

____ (10) *Kicking game* (vary the daily emphasis).

____ (x) Fourth-quarter drill (sprints).

Makeup work for absentees.

Diagram 6-7

SCRIMMAGE BREAKDOWN SCHEDULE

August and Spring Drills

Time (Min) Time-Block

____ (15) *Warmup Period.*

____ (20) *Receivers:* Individual pass routes.

Line: Blocking patterns.

Diagram 6-7 Continued

____ (20) *Secondary:* Live perimeter.

DL & LB's: Techniques & coverages.

____ (5) Break.

____ (20) *Half-Line Scrimmages* (slot side & tight side vs. divided varsity defense).

Note: Separate the 2 groups by a 10-yard dummy barrier. Starting offensive backfield alternates from SS to TS with each play. Two centers and two backside guards are required, plus two defensive nose guards or middle linebackers.

____ (10) Break (Reserve squads begin a separate scrimmage).

____ (20) *Half-Line Scrimmages* (Continue routine, except swap sides for offensive slot side and tight side).

—Alternate Plan—

A forty-minute game type scrimmage with chains & downmarker can substitute for a half-line breakdown scrimmage. Divide the best athletes and allow a 10-minute break after first 20 minutes.

SEASON SCHEDULES
Diagram 6-8

MONDAY (w/o pads)

Time (Min) Time-Block

____ (xx) Film.

____ (xx) Instructions.

____ (15) *Warmup Period.*

____ (30) *Kicking-Game Review.*

____ (30) *Secondary* (Select) Man coverage drills; tackling technique; perimeter work (scout report).

DL & LB's: Scout report and tackling technique (dummy).

Diagram 6-8 Continued

___ (5) *Break*

___ (10) *Backfield:* New plays or timing work.

        Linemen: Blocking patterns or pass protection.

___ (10) *Running Under Punts* (6 lines).

___ (20) *Receivers:* Pass patterns.

        Linemen: Sled work.

___ (5) *Point After Touchdown* (PAT).

___ (xx) Individual help time to upgrade technique (voluntary).

Diagram 6-9

TUESDAY (Heavy Day)

Time (Min) Time-Block

___ (xx) Film.

___ (xx) Instructions.

___ (15) *Warmup Period.*

___ (10) *Backs:* Climb blocking.

        Linemen: Sled work.

___ (20) *Receivers:* Pass patterns (live vs. opponent's type coverage).

        Linemen: Blocking patterns (vs. opponent's alignments).

___ (20) *Secondary:* Perimeter drill (vs. opponent's pass patterns).

        DL & LB's: Breakdown drills or Scout report (best opponent plays).

___ (5) Break

___ (20) *Team Defense.*

___ (10) *Challenge Offense.*

___ (10) *Open Offense.*

___ (10) *Punting* (live).

___ (xx) 4th quarter drill (Supplement: consider a short scrimmage in place of sprints, for those who did not play in Friday's game).

Diagram 6-10

WEDNESDAY (Med-Heavy Day)

Time (Min) Time-Block

____ (xx) Instructions.

____ (15) *Warmup Period.*

____ (15) *Backs:* Play polish and tackling techniques (separated groups).

Linemen: Sled work.

____ (20) *Receivers:* Pass patterns (skeleton, for timing).

Linemen: Blocking patterns and/or pass blocking.

____ (20) *Secondary:* Perimeter drill (vs. opponent's pass patterns).

DL & LB's: Scout report (live reaction to opponent's blocking combinations and pet plays).

____ (5) Break.

____ (10) *Kick-off and returns.*

____ (10) *Punt returns.*

____ (15) *Team offensive review.*

____ (15) *Team defensive review.*

____ (xx) 4th quarter drill.

Diagram 6-11

THURSDAY (w/o pads)

Time (Min) Time-Block

____ (xx) Final Instructions (trip plans).

____ (15) *Light Warmup Period.*

____ (15) *Play polish by teams.*

____ (30) *Review entire kicking game* (conclude with PAT's).

____ (xx) View a film, if needed.

EXPLANATORY REMARKS

1. Normal workouts are planned for a two-hour duration.
2. Our time-blocks are designed for a two-platoon system to accomodate a thirty-five to forty member varsity, with a minimum of four coaches, in which almost all athletes are taught both offense and defense. To give built-in depth to

capable and ready athletes, the starting offense becomes the second-team defense, theoretically, and the starting defense becomes the second-team offense. Specialists exist, however, on both the offensive and defensive teams. Our remaining squadsmen are assigned to the junior varsity team, which is guided by an assigned staff.

3. If the varsity is divided entirely into offensive and defensive teams, you can nearly double the instructional time spent on all speciality areas.

4. If the junior varsity is a part of the varsity squad, you should make allowances for JV scrimmages and kicking-game work during the varsity's team offensive drills.

SCRIMMAGE GUIDELINES

1. A "quick whistle" is used in all team contact work, to limit the players' exposure to injuries.

2. During the season, you should discourage tackling to the ground and emphasize a defensive "lock-up and release."

3. Designate the scout-squad quarterback as "sacred" from hard contact by a physically superior varsity defense. The important point of concern is to protect the physical and mental well-being of everyone, to develop self-confidence in the inexperienced quarterbacks, and to be able to execute the ball-handling mechanics of the plays involved in the weekly scout report.

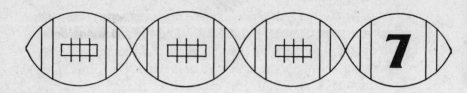

COACHING POINTERS
FOR BACKS AND RECEIVERS

As a prerequisite to the remaining chapters, which cover the keystone offense and its enrichment plays, certain backfield and receiver fundamentals need reviewing. Their purpose is to provide fundamental groundwork and to eliminate heavy rhetoric and subsequent repetition when discussing offensive-play assignments.

These coaching generalities will give pertinent tips for the improvement of all backfield and receiver techniques. Some of the areas covered are (1) stance, (2) ball handling, (3) faking, (4) footwork, (5) running form, (6) blocking approach, (7) passing, (8) catching, and (9) releasing from the scrimmage line on pass routes. Psychological factors are included.

POINTERS FOR THE FULLBACK

1. Take a balanced 3-point stance, 3 yards from the line of scrimmage, as a recommended starting point. You must be close enough to strike the neutral zone at the moment of blocking contact on any quick-opener play. (The actual depth in the backfield will vary in proportion to the speed of the individual). Your feet should be straight across, without a stagger, and kept parallel. If right handed, place that hand on the ground with slight pressure on the tripod fingers. Rest your other forearm on its close knee.

2. Never point or lean from your stance.

3. Always step with the near foot. Never cross-over step to reach a play hole.

4. Receive all hand-offs from the quarterback with your inside elbow raised up, with its adjacent hand facing down in a fail-safe, "catcher" position.

5. Explode at the assigned hole whether receiving the football or faking.

6. Hit quickly into the play hole with explosive force on all direct hand-off plays. Either square-up into the hole, or break at a decisive angle *after* (not before) receiving the hand-off.

7. Follow behind the path of your trapping guard on trap plays, and square-up into the play hole. Stay in the running alley where you receive blocking support.

8. If called upon to carry the football on a fullback wedge play, follow deliberately behind your wedging linemen, striding *patiently* until a void appears.

9. Place a soft arm-fold over the football during the quarterback's faking stage, during any fullback-fake play, and give a convincing plunge into the line.

10. Drop your inside shoulder during a play-fake, and "ham it up"—get tackled or find a block. Fill for your pulling guard at his vacated position on bootleg passes and reverse plays, and fill for your tackle when he pulls from the line on a Tackle Trap play. Seal off any defensive penetration!

11. Block defensive ends with a controlled approach, using choppy steps from a wide foot-base. Keep body weight at your command, so that an adjustment step can be taken laterally to compensate for any change of direction by the opponent.

POINTERS FOR THE TAILBACK

1. Take a balanced, 2-point stance, 1 yard directly behind the fullback. Never crowd the fullback because you need the room to angle into an opening that may appear within the battle zone. Your feet must be parallel, your head held up, and body weight should be forward on the balls of the feet. Turn your thumbs inside your knees, with elbows facing outward to maintain a ready position. Do not rest: be alert to move instantly on the snap of the football.

2. Never point or lean from your stance!

3. On straight-hitting plays, step with your nearside foot. Do not take a cross-over or false step. A counter step is necessary on certain misdirection plays.

4. Step laterally on wide plays, and drive at the outside leg of your lead blocker on inside plays.

5. Receive all ball exchanges with your inside elbow in a raised position, with its adjacent hand facing down as a "catcher hand."

6. Carry out all play fakes: this includes keepers, options and play-action passes that involve you in a fake hand-off of the ball.

7. Break off the tail of your lead blocker on linebacker isolation, lead, and off-tackle plays, once you get into the attack area.

8. On off-tackle plays, *get as much as you can* at the point of attack before cutting for daylight. As a general guideline, follow your key blocker to the hole first, then seek out cut-back openings against-the-grain. Remember, clever daylight runners do not wander aimlessly—the shortest path to the goal line always will be a straight course.

9. Quickly get into a proper pitch relationship with your quarterback on option plays. A prime option advantage from an I-formation is that the tailback can gain a wide pitch relationship instantly, without delaying the internal mechanics of the play. Always achieve the ideal pitch relationship 4 yards deep from your quarterback and 3 yards to his outside.

10. Block defensive ends with a controlled approach from a wide foot-base. Use choppy steps to keep your speed in check and your body weight at your command. When pass blocking against a 5-man line, the tailback usually functions as a supporting blocker to his fullback.

POINTERS FOR THE SLOT BACK AND SPLIT END

1. Take a balanced, 3-point stance. If right-handed, stagger your right toe behind the left heel. Place your right hand

on the ground with enough pressure on the tripod fingers for a quick thrust forward. Rest your left forearm on the left knee.

2. Never point, lean sideways, or take a false step before or during your initial take-off.

3. Receive ball exchanges from the quarterback with your nearside elbow up and your "catcher hand" down when running slot-back misdirection or end-around plays. With trap blocking, the slot back must break sharp up the running lane, behind the block of his trapping tackle or guard.

4. Sprint quickly to attain the assigned pitch relationship with your quarterback, when involved in a slot-back option or end-around pitch. Proper depth and all-out effort is necessary in getting a sideline advantage at the farside corner.

5. Explode off the line of scrimmage from your starting stance, as would a sprinter, on all upfield assignments.

6. Pose a threat to the defense every time you release off the line, creating fear and respect as a potential receiver in every play. With constant pressure applied upon the defense, you will become a more effective blocker and decoy. Always be a 100 percent football player by hustling on every play.

7. Experiment with your defender on backside plays, so that you can later exploit his weaknesses. Penetrate deep within the creases which divide the coverage areas, and carry out your acrossfield blocking-assignment. Determine how you are covered—carelessly, with overplaying, etc. Backside assignments must be taken seriously.

8. Get the most out of your pass routes by developing precision footwork. With the exception of angle-in routes, begin by driving your defender straight backward to create a large "cushion." Then collect your weight while slowing to three-fourths speed during the control stage of your route, before making the final cut. As the final cut is made, break sharply to get a leverage advantage laterally, or to the inside or outside shoulder of your opponent.

a. Develop your timing through repetition on a marked field.

b. Learn precision by emphasizing consistency in running your route. Learning to stay on course and running at a steady pace during preliminary movements will help you acquire polish in your technique and maneuvers.

9. Master all the finer points of pass receiving. Becoming a good pass receiver involves more than just catching a football. Continually practice the proper techniques of (1) exploding off the line, (2) jockeying your defender out of position, (3) executing sharp footwork, (4) placing your hands together properly during each pass reception, and (5) carrying out your team's play assignments. To be outstanding, you have to master *all* of these areas. After all, *anyone* can run up the field, but only a trained receiver can out-think and whip his defensive coverage, outhustle his opponent, and become a scoring threat on every play.

a. Make all faking movements with your head, shoulder, and hips prior to your final cut. Avoid disrupting the normal timing of your route with free-lance or stop-and-go footwork that consumes extra time.

b. Make all final cuts distinct to force a positive separation from your defender, either in front of or beyond him, plus a bonus step or two advantage.

c. Make necessary adjustments in the depth of your pass routes, by requesting specific time-beat pass releases from your quarterback on designated patterns. You can prevent the defensive secondary from matching its alignment depth to that of your route breaks, simply by communicating with your quarterback to vary the time-beat of your final cuts.

10. "Break" your route after the final cut, then find an open area if your quarterback gets into pass-rush trouble and has to scramble out of his pocket.

11. Go to meet the football on all passes. The longer the ball lingers in the air, the greater the risk of an interception.

12. "Look" the football all the way into your hands when receiving a thrown pass. Do *not* take your eyes off the ball during the last split second. Pull the elbows inward, relax your fingers, make a catching basket with your hands, and allow some "give" with your hands and fingers as the ball is entrapped. Concentration, relaxation, and belief in yourself make the winning difference: "I can do it!" should be your heartfelt statement of confidence.

13. Catch the football with your hands either thumbs-in or thumbs-out. Avoid cradling the football against your body.
    a. *Thumbs-in catch:* Used to receive any pass thrown at chest height or above, while you are turned and facing the ball in flight. Reception of the ball in flight, at chest level on a Curl-route, would necessitate a thumbs-in pass catch. Do not use a thumbs-in position of the hands to catch an upfield pass from overhead, *unless* it is necessary to turn and face the ball in flight.
    b. *Thumbs-out catch:* Used to receive any pass thrown (1) below the waist or (2) directly over your head while running a downfield route. This technique is therefore used on most pass receptions. The fingers should be kept well-spread and flexible.

14. Make certain you tuck the ball away properly before running with it. Lock the points of the ball in the crook of your arm at one end and in your folded fingers at the opposite end. Never raise the elbow upward while running, since the ball can then lose its body support and drop to the ground.

15. Defeat defensive hold-up tactics by fighting to the outside.
    a. Take one quick step directly at the defender, to influence him into taking a backward step, then release outside. If bumped repeatedly by the defender, give him a forearm flipper and fight to the outside.
    b. Take one step forward with your outside foot and reverse-pivot on that foot to the outside. If aligned on the right side, pivot on your right foot and swing the left arm to aid the momentum of the reverse-pivot. If on the left side, pivot on your left foot and swing the right arm.

c. As a change-up tactic, fake inside and break to the outside.

d. On occasion, you may have to fake outside and break to the inside *if* your assignment is to release into an inside zone crease.

COACHING POINTERS FOR THE QUARTERBACK

RUNNING PLAYS

1. Take a comfortable stance under the center, with a natural bend in your knees. Keep your head up, your back flat and your thumbs together with hands eagled. Lift upward with slight pressure under the center's crotch for (1) exchange security, and (2) a reference point to the center for an accurate snap of the football.

2. Check both left and right sides of the line for correct alignment and stillness, before beginning your cadence. Never tip off a play by swaying, pointing, looking, or glancing at the attack area during cadence. Guard against any give-away habits! Have a set routine in checking the offensive line during the semi-automatic number call, then keep your head and eyes fixed straight ahead during the remainder of the cadence.

3. Bark out the cadence in gruff, sharp tones. Be decisive in your carriage, mannerisms, play call, and command of the team at the line of scrimmage.

4. Form a mental image of how you wish to perform, hold it in your subconscious and carry it onto the playing field. Always work at being yourself, however, and strive to develop your own personality. Acquire a readiness to relate to all your teammates. When you build confidence from within, it will breed confidence in others!

5. Fold your hands under the football as it is snapped from center and then pull it immediately into your "third hand" or stomach.

6. Use a front-out step with your nearside foot on fullback hand-offs and fake-and-give plays. A front-out technique is used on play-action passes off a fake of the fullback Base

play—and also on bootleg pass plays—with a reverse-pivot following the initial step of the bootleg.

7. Use a reverse-pivot (spin) technique on direct hand-offs to the tailback, pivoting as deeply as possible in the backfield when making the ball exchange. A deep hand-off gives your tailback added opportunity for daylight running. The same reverse-out technique is used on play-action passes off the fake of the off-tackle power play.

8. "Look" the football into the receiving back's third-hand when making a hand-off exchange. Execute a fake-and-keep, a fake-and-give or a fake-and-pass *exactly* the same way each time. Place emphasis on keeping the defense uncertain. Clever faking will give potency to your offense, so develop yourself into a ball-handling magician.

9. Go directly to the short corner when executing a standard keep-or-pitch option on a defensive end. Achieve depth in the backfield first, then pressure the end to commit his option-play intentions, never allowing yourself to be outwitted by feathering tactics. If a play fake is used, give a convincing hand-off movement with your arms and hands, to curtail defensive pursuit before applying option pressure.

PASSING PLAYS

1. Set up quickly into your pass pocket behind the tackle.
   a. After receiving the ball snap and stepping away from the center, complete any necessary play fake and then get as much *depth* as possible into your pocket. Remember, your pull-up is timed one count prior to the time-beat release of your pass pattern.
   b. Hide the football in your high chest area, concealing it on your retreat into the pocket. Protect the ball with both hands!
   c. Plant the outside (rear) foot to bring your momentum to a halt as you reach the timed depth of your pocket.
      (1) If you are a right-handed passer, your pull-up behind the tackle to the right side will be brought in check by a plant of your right foot before squaring-up to the line of scrimmage.

(2) As a right-handed passer, your pull-up in the pocket to the left side will be brought in check by a plant and pivot of your left foot so that you can square-up to the line of scrimmage.

d. Stand tall in your pocket after setting-up. Do not telegraph the pass by watching any one receiver: look straight into the group of receivers that make up your first option. Quickly scan the defensive pick-up of the receivers in your first option, being aware of the secondary receivers. Most patterns in the Slot-I format will have two or more receivers within the quarterback's line of view.

2. Evaluate your ball grip and index-finger position to improve your accuracy.

a. Place the point of your little finger where it touches the near center of the lace, allowing a slight space between your palm and the football to aid in finger-tip control. Place the other hand along the opposite side of the ball for support.

b. Position your index finger enough to the rear of the football to help it keep its nose-up trajectory on a deep pass. A soft, nose-up trajectory is somewhat easier to handle on a pass reception. A grip favoring the back end of the football is essential for small hands, and is also helpful in controlling a tendency to overthrow. A tendency to underthrow, likewise, can be partially corrected by assuming a higher index-finger position on the ball.

c. Bring the ball up to a *high* chest level as you square to the line. Do not let your attention be diverted to the defensive pass rushers, as this is a major cause of interceptions being thrown.

3. Develop a consistent release of the football.

a. Put self-discipline and patience into practice when working on pull-up footwork, ball grip, the timing of your ball release, and stepping decisively in the direction of your throw. Always consider your natural talents, but learn all you can about the art of throwing a football. If you begin to experience problems in accuracy, you can usually trace the source back to basic footwork, grip, timing, and the proper step of the lead foot in the direction of the throw.

b. Pull the ball up *behind the ear* at the start of your throwing motion. This is basic quarterback mechanics. A baseball pitcher's style of dropping the ball below hip level creates problems in achieving desirable hand rotation, index finger release and, therefore, overall accuracy when passing a football. The elbow of your passing arm should have a natural bend, should be raised to shoulder level and positioned straight-out in line with your chest, and parallel to the ground.

c. Take a lead step with your left foot (right-handed passer) directly at the intended receiver at the start of the throwing motion.

d. Take advantage of the benefit gained from a driving push-off by the rear foot and hip during your release. This may not come naturally, so you may have to work at its development. At the completion of your pass release, your rear foot should move slightly forward.

e. Release the football from behind the ear to achieve a strong whip of the ball as it leaves your hand. As the ball is released, the elbow of the passing arm should be slightly forward while the other arm gives necessary body balance.

f. Snap the ball and palm of your hand downward upon release. This action will allow the football to leave the top of the index finger properly.

g. Release high passes slightly beyond the shoulder, and direct passes in front of the shoulder.

h. Make certain that your throwing motion has a continual follow-through toward the target, allowing the wrist and index finger to *flop* toward the receiver: never allow your wrist to turn clockwise. As the ball is released, allow the passing arm to naturally swing slightly across your body in its follow-through movement.

i. Never throw cross-body during your release of the football! Always throw "in line with your spine." With the proper square-up and placement of your lead foot during the throw, you should never have a problem of throwing off-balance or against your body symmetry.

j. Learn to know your receiver's traits on the practice field, so that you can improve upon your percentage of completions. Familarity is a mutual aid in improving all time-beat receptions. Because timing is ever important, don't wait for a receiver to get a "wide open" separation from his opponent, since a delay may lead to an interception when the ball is released too late.

4. Develop your ability to concentrate while in the heat of battle.
   a. Keep your poise by staying on balance and ignoring defensive distractions.
   b. Learn to throw to a predetermined "spot" as your chosen receiver makes his cut.
   c. Generally aim your passes head level at your receivers.
   d. Pass between linebackers with a straight spiral whenever possible. However, if you sense the danger of a linebacker interception, then release the ball with an extra arch in its flight (judgement decision).
   e. Repeat your pass-delivery technique until it is part of your "conditioned reflexes." Concentrate on your timed release and polish your form with the following ritual: set-up quickly, square your shoulders and feet properly, scan your option selections, step at your target choice with the lead foot, and fire the football instantly.

5. Use a change-up in delivery, to coincide with the angular depth and width of individual routes and your receiver's relationship within the opponent's pass coverage.
   a. Use a *bullet* pass on split-end Trail, Curl, Quick and Out routes (See Diagram 7-1); on slot back Fan, Scissor and Cross routes (See Diagram 7-2); on tight-end Curl, Crease and Drag routes, and on a tailback Flare route (See Diagram 7-3). A bullet pass is accomplished by using a downward snap of the wrist with an exaggerated follow-through.

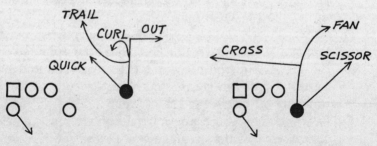

Diagram 7-1   Diagram 7-2

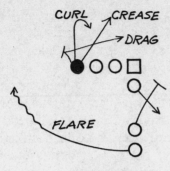

Diagram 7-3

b. Use a *floating* pass on split end Post, Go, Snake, Flag, and deep Fan routes (See Diagram 7-4); on slot back "X" and Scissor and Up routes (See Diagram 7-5); on tight end Drive, In and Out, Railroad and "X" routes, and on a tailback Flare and Up route (See Diagram 7-6). A floating pass is accomplished by releasing the football slightly beyond shoulder level, which is higher or sooner than the release of a bullet pass. An upward arc is necessary, which is the type of pass that a receiver can run underneath.

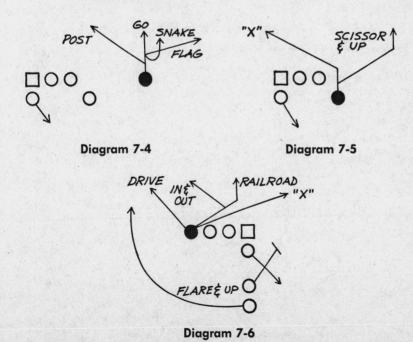

Diagram 7-4   **Diagram 7-5**

Diagram 7-6

c. Use a *lob* pass on a slot back or tight-end Quick route (See Diagram 7-7) and on tailback Screen-routes (See Diagram 7-8). The intensity of a lob pass is determined by the distance and mobility of the receiver, and the location of the linebackers. When used on a Quick route, the ball can usually be released softly enough to hang into the receiver's hands while he is on the run. When used on tailback Screen-passes, more zip should be placed on the ball because of the pursuit hazard endangering a near stationary receiver.

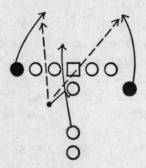 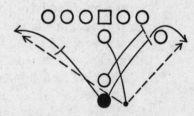

Diagram 7-7 Quick Route   **Diagram 7-8 Tailback Screen**

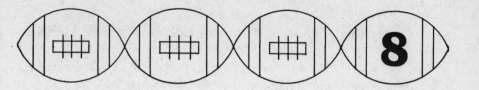

KEYSTONE OFFENSE
OF THE SLOT-I

The keystone offense is the heart and soul of our system since it binds together all the principles and beliefs in which we place our trust. In our keystone structure, the quarterback functions as the keystone athlete, because he helps coordinate the offense and thereby makes it possible to balance our run-pass ratio.

Without a sound, complete, yet simple offensive arrangement, it would be difficult to have a stable offensive program, regardless of all the high-level planning, fundamental teaching and hard labor. A keystone offense must be more than an assortment of plays. It should be resourceful with plays complementing themselves in a mixture of series, and it should exemplify the philosphy of its designer.

In order to organize the various play concepts of the Slot-I's keystone offense, all interwoven segments of the attack have been divided into a "fullback sequence" and "tailback sequence" categories, so that you will see how certain plays relate to other plays within their series. But, keep in mind that a Slot-I offense is not just a play-series attack. Chapters 2 and 3 have pointed out numerous ways to apply alternating pressure on the opposing defense to keep it loose, vunerable and in a state of uncertainty.

Table 8-I

A Categorized Illustration of the Keystone Running and Passing Structure

Keystone Running Game (12 plays)	Keystone Passing Game (12 patterns)
(Fullback Sequence)	(Slot Side Pull-Up)
2-1 Base	16-15 Pass: 2-1 Base Pass: 6-5
2-1 Base Option	Power Pass:
2-1 Quick Trap	Fan
3-4 Cross Trap	Divide
5-6 Trap	Scissor
(Tailback Sequence)	Scissor and Up
2-1 (4-3) Isolate	"X"
2-1 (4-3) Isolate Keep-or-Option	Cross
21-22 Tackle Trap	See-Saw
6-5 Power	16-15 Pass, Screen Right-
16-15 Lead Option	Screen Left-
8-7 Sweep	Screen Middle
1-2 Draw	(Slot or Tight-Side Play-Action)
	2-1 Base, Quick Pass
	(Tight Side Bootleg-Action)
	Waggle Pass Left (Right)

A DIAGRAMED ILLUSTRATION OF THE KEYSTONE RUNNING AND PASSING STRUCTURE (FROM A SLOT-RIGHT FORMATION).

Diagram 8-1

A REVIEW OF BASE-BLOCKING ASSIGNMENTS FOR LINEMEN

Base blocking assignments have three areas of recognition:

(1) Inside

(2) Over

(3) Outside

Explanation:

(1) If a defender is aligned to your *inside*, block him. (The center and backside guard must protect their onside gap).

(2) If no one is there (N/T), block the defender aligned directly *over* you.

(3) N/T, block the nearest defender aligned to your *outside*.

Additional Assignments:

(1) Special blocking patterns are used predominately in the Slot-I's running attack.

(2) Base-blocking rules apply to any blocker that is not involved in a blocking pattern.

THE OFFENSIVE ATTACK

Now we shall venture into the keystone play book. All running plays and pass patterns are illustrated from a slot right and slot left formation, against a variety of chosen defensive fronts and perimeters. Assignments and points of emphasis will accompany each set of plays and patterns.

COMMENTS: (Diagram 8-2) 2-1 BASE

The middle Base play is the quickest hitting of all Slot-I plays. Its spontaneous outburst, combined with a good fire-out by the line, will often catch the inside defense unprepared.

This play is used often to set up the remainder of our fullback belly series, but it has its best gains when sprung by surprise after a succession of tailback plays. Desperation "hand tackling" by the defense seldom stops this play when it is used on a quick count.

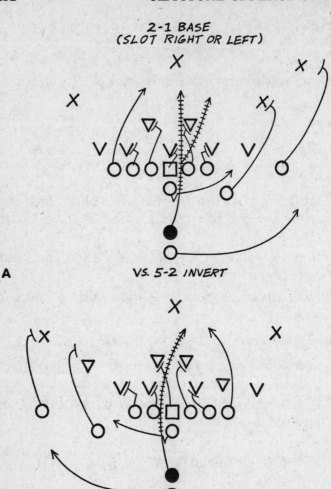

2-1 BASE
(SLOT RIGHT OR LEFT)

A   VS. 5-2 INVERT

B   VS. SPLIT-4

Diagram 8-2

In short yardage situations, a wedge block can be called in the huddle (Chapter 4).

ASSIGNMENTS:

Play-side

End	Force DHB.
Tackle	Base rule. Block outside vs. a Split-4 type defense.

| Guard | Base rule. |
| Center | Base rule (Split-4, block play-side LB) whenever N/T, block backside LB). |

Backside

Guard	Base rule (first man inside center). Loop block a Split-4.
Tackle	Base rule (sustain the block). Loop block a Split-4.
End	Crease.

Slot Back   Play-side—force safety.
Backside—split crease (block #2).

Fullback   Explode directly into the play hole. If area is congested, break after receiving the ball.

Tailback   Swing play-side.

Quarterback   Receive the snap, front-out with a short step with your close foot, and give a jab hand-off to FB. Carry out the option fake to the corner.

COMMENTS: (Diagram 8-3) 2-1 BASE OPTION

The Base Option is an extension of the middle Base play and is a very reliable segment of the belly series. A fake of the quick-opener up the middle from an "I" backfield tends to hold the interior defense better than an extended-arm fake to the fullback through the guard-tackle hole. The Base Option is also simpler to execute than a veer option from an "I" alignment, is less time-consuming, and is practically error-free.

The fullback fulfills a major role in the play's success by freezing the defense with a hand-off fake and then helping to block the nearby linebacker. The quarterback is instructed to think in terms of pitching the ball first and running it second.

Forcing tactics by the play-side receivers against a pass-conscious secondary is well-suited for this type of option. The Base Option is run at best advantage to the tight side if it can be used opposite a perimeter rotation, but toward a wide (flex) slot against a Split-4 or 5-3 type of defense, with zone-pass coverage.

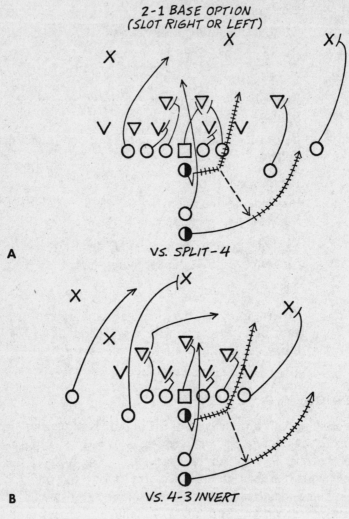

2-1 BASE OPTION
(SLOT RIGHT OR LEFT)

A   VS. SPLIT-4

B   VS. 4-3 INVERT

Diagram 8-3

ASSIGNMENTS:
Play-side

End	Force DHB, stalk and block. TE must block inside against a "loaded" 8-man front such as found in a Split-6, Wide-Tackle 6 or Gap-8 defense.
Tackle	Base rule.
Guard	Base rule.

Center	Base rule.

Backside

Guard	Base rule. Loop block a Split-4.
Tackle	Base rule—3 counts and release. Loop block a Split-4.
End	Crease.

Slot Back Play-side—force, stalk and block the rover-back or inside safety. Flex into a wide slot against 8-man alignments, such as a Split-4(6) or 5-3, etc., and block the walk-away end or OLB. Backside—Split crease (block #2).

Fullback Explode directly into onside center-guard gap with a convincing play fake. Influence the defense as much as possible, and find someone to block. If the ILB is located in the center-guard area, you are responsible for eliminating him from pursuit.

Tailback Swing toward the play-side wide corner, keeping a pitch relationship with QB, 4 yards deep and 3 yards to his outside. If QB turns upfield, then turn upfield with him, keeping a pitch relationship.

Quarterback Receive snap, front-out with a short step on your close foot, and give a pronounced jab fake to FB. Now, continue along the line, rounding slightly outside the offensive tackle and remain ever-prepared to option-pitch the football.

Standarized Coaching Pointers:

1. Make the DE commit his intentions. Run on a course through his inside shoulder. If he lingers, try a premature fake pitch, then make your decision either to turn upfield or to pitch the football.
2. Keep your option decision simple. Think "yes" or "no." Remember, the QB must option the DE—not vice versa.
3. Think in terms of pitching the football to eliminate indecision. Flip the ball to the

trailing tailback, if and when the DE commits to you.
4. Make something positive happen: never allow the defense to string the play out to the wide corner.

COMMENTS: (Diagram 8-4) 2-1 QUICK TRAP

The fullback Quick Trap is one of the more explosive plays in the Slot-I attack, and it fits perfectly into the belly-play deception scheme. With the fullback taking a cut-back step up the middle behind his pulling guard, the Quick Trap takes on a characteristic of an inside counter, and often a linebacker isolation play. If the defense holds a size advantage, quickness and angle-blocking technique can serve as an equalizer and also help to discourage the opponent from attempting forceful penetration into the offensive backfield. As an enrichment play, a trap option could be included to capitalize on the defensive commitment to stop the inside trap.

ASSIGNMENTS:

Play-side

End	TE: block acrossfield on near safety. SE: force.
Tackle	Base rule (responsible for ILB on Split-4).
Guard	Inside rule; unless the opponent is trap target, block outside.
Center	Block backside.

Backside

Guard	Pull from the line behind center and trap the first opponent to appear in the play-side center-guard hole. The target may be a lineman or ILB.
Tackle	Fill for the pulling guard; if N/A, apply the base rule.
End	Crease.
Slot Back	Play-side: force. Backside: crease.
Fullback	Explode directly at the awayside guard and receive the hand-off with the inside elbow up. Then take an inside cut-back step to follow behind the

trapping guard, breaking off his buttocks as the trap block is made.

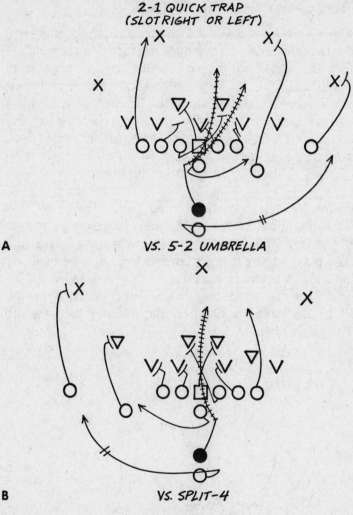

2-1 QUICK TRAP
(SLOT RIGHT OR LEFT)

A   *VS. 5-2 UMBRELLA*

B   *VS. SPLIT-4*

Diagram 8-4

Tailback	Take a quick step to the awayside, then counter step laterally to the play-side. Carry out the fake of a trap option.
Quarterback	Receive the snap, front-out with a short step to the awayside with the close foot, and give a jab

hand-off to FB. Reverse-around without delay and carry out an option fake with TB.

COMMENTS: (Diagram 8-5) 3-4 CROSS TRAP

The Cross Trap gives the Slot-I offense a necessary misdirection play for the tailback. It represents a revitalized version of a T-formation crossbuck, which is one of the original plays from football's early history. The basic intention of the play is unchanged: its design is meant to draw the defense inward with a fullback fake to the opposite side of the play. Trap blocking benefits the play's execution by making it possible for small linemen to open up a clear running lane for the tailback. As a supplement to trap blocking, X and Y-blocking also can be used (ie., 3 Cross-X; 4 Cross-Y, etc.).

To realize the full potential of the Cross Trap play, the quarterback and tailback must have the necessary patience to fake decisively. The quarterback must give a convincing jab-fake of a fullback Base play, while a distinct counter step must be made by the delaying tailback before he breaks across and follows behind his trapping guard to reach the play hole. Sleight of hand by the quarterback in concealing the ball from the defense greatly adds to the effectiveness of the play.

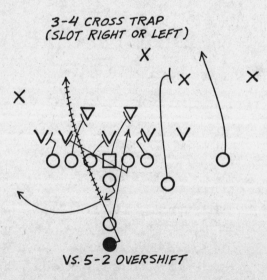

3-4 CROSS TRAP
(SLOT RIGHT OR LEFT)

A   VS. 5-2 OVERSHIFT

Diagram 8-5

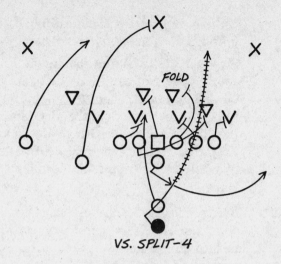

B
VS. SPLIT–4

Diagram 8-5 Continued

ASSIGNMENTS:

Play-side

End	TE: block the base rule. SE: force.
Tackle	Inside rule; if N/A, block outside (may fold block a Split-4).
Guard	Base rule unless LB is over, then block inside (may fold block on Split-4 LB).
Center	Over; if N/A, block backside.

Backside

Guard	Pull from the line behind the center and trap the first defender outside the offensive tackle.
Tackle	Base rule: 3 counts and release. Loop block a Split-4.
End	Crease.
Slot Back	Play-side: base rule (turn the opponent outward); if facing a Split-4, take a wide (flex) alignment and force the OLB upfield. Backside: split crease (block #2).
Fullback	Drive into the center-guard gap, opposite the play-side. Give a convincing plunge into the line,

with an exaggerated shoulder-dipping fake, and
fill-block for the pulling guard.

Tailback   Step behind the path of the driving FB with the
counter-side foot as a delay measure during the
QB-FB play fake. Then step toward the play-side
trap hole with the opposite foot. Sprint behind
the QB for the ball exchange and follow behind
the path of the trapping guard. Drive through the
play hole and sprint into the northbound running
lane.

Quarterback   Receive the snap,, make a short front-out step
with your close foot, and give a convincing jab-
fake to FB. Then pivot around off your inside
foot, placing your back to the line of scrimmage,
and hand the ball forward to the crossing TB for
the ball exchange. Carry out the fake of a keeper
around the end.

COMMENTS: (Diagram 8-6) 5-6 TRAP

The off-tackle Trap is the fullback's outside belly play from the
Slot-I. Many coaches consider a play of this type an essential
element of a winning offensive attack. A simple play to execute, the
off-tackle trap can slip through the line for long pains against a
forcing type of defensive front. From a centralized alignment, the
fullback trap can hit the off-tackle hole to either side, with the same
directness and quickness that a slant play can hit from a full "T."
Although it can be used with some degree of success against any
defensive alignment, it has its best advantage against a 7-man front
in which better blocking angles exist.

ASSIGNMENTS:

Play-side

End   TE: Block inside rule; if N/T, block over (5-3,
etc). SE: shield block.

Tackle   Inside rule; if N/T, block over (Wide-Tackle 6,
etc).

Guard   Pull from the line and trap the onside DE.

Center   Base rule (check play-side gap).

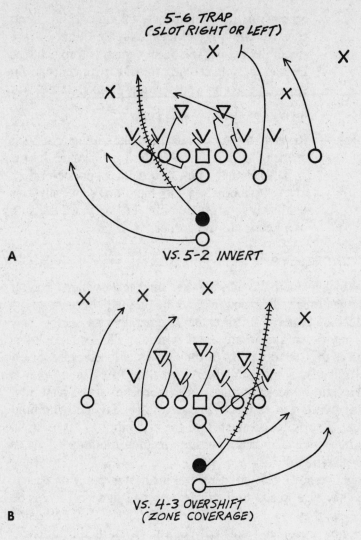

5-6 TRAP
(SLOT RIGHT OR LEFT)

A VS. 5-2 INVERT

B VS. 4-3 OVERSHIFT
(ZONE COVERAGE)

Diagram 8-6

Backside

Guard	Base rule.
Tackle	Base rule: 3 counts and release. Loop block a Split-4.
End	Crease.

Slot Back   Play-side: block inside rule; if N/T, block over (5-3, etc). Backside: crease.

Fullback	Step with the onside foot, taking a slight bend toward the play-side off-tackle lane. Drive forcefully behind the pulling guard's trap block as he makes contact with the DE. Concentrate on springing free as you separate from the line.
Tailback	Swing toward play-side corner.
Quarterback	Receive the snap, then front-out with an extended stride to gain depth in the backfield. Meet the FB at the exchange point as quickly as possible, then give the football a jab hand-off. Conceal your hands on your outside hip and carry out the fake of a keeper to the corner.

COMMENTS: (Diagram 8-7) 2-1 (4-3) ISOLATE

The Isolate is football's all-purpose "linebacker wham" play. It is one of the finer inside power-plays in football, because of its unique blocking pattern. It is acclaimed generally as a reliable play to use on any down and in any field position. The Isolate play is considered as the starting point of the Slot-I's tailback-belly series.

The fullback is a key blocker in making the Isolate play a success. His climb block, on the inside linebacker at the play-side, is vital in giving the tailback his necessary daylight running-opportunity. The fullback must have the capability to "take on" a quick-reading linebacker who attempts to plug the attack hole as the play is diagnosed.

A double-team block often results inside the point of attack, since the play-side guard and tackle reject or ignore the inside linebacker as they apply their base-blocking rule. The inside linebacker now becomes "isolated" for the block of the fullback, which is how the play-name originated.

As an aid to the offensive linemen, the quarterback makes his play-call number at the approximate location of the linebacker (1 and 2 or 3 and 4 holes). If the defensive structure has caused confusion or if there is difficulty otherwise, a supplemental 3 or 4 hole Lead play can be called to utilize base blocking, with the fullback serving as a clean-up blocker through the play-side dive hole.

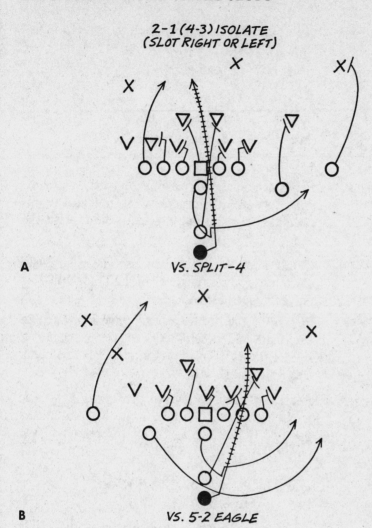

2-1 (4-3) ISOLATE
(SLOT RIGHT OR LEFT)

A   VS. SPLIT-4

B   VS. 5-2 EAGLE

Diagram 8-7

ASSIGNMENTS:

Play-side

End   TE: block over or outside (turn the opponent outward). SE: force.

Tackle   Ignore the LB and apply the base rule (block inside if covered by a LB).

| Guard | Ignore the LB and apply the base rule (double-team a 5-2 nose guard). |
| Center | Over; N/T, backside LB. |

Backside

Guard	Base rule (block the down lineman vs. a Split-4).
Tackle	Base rule (block outside vs. a Split-4).
End	Crease.
Slot Back	Play-side: block over or outside (turn the opponent outward). Backside: swing toward the opposite flank, assuming a pitch position with the QB.
Fullback	Climb block the ILB. If defense makes an 8-gap shift, lead toward the dive hole and block the free defender outside the tackle.
Tailback	Step with the onside foot, receive ball deep in backfield, and forcefully drive through the attack hole. Follow the inside leg of your FB and break clean off his block.
Quarterback	Receive the snap, reverse pivot and hand the football off to the TB as deep in the backfield as possible. Carry out a fake of the option to the corner.

COMMENTS: (Diagram 8-8) 2-1 (4-3) ISOLATE KEEP
OR OPTION

The Isolate Keep—or—Option is an extension of the inside Isolate play, and like the Base Option, it is reliable and reasonably safe to execute. The fullback again plays a key blocking role by helping to eliminate the inside linebacker from lateral pursuit. Since the defense has a tendency to collapse internally against the Isolate play (due to its deep and deliberate hand-off exchange), a buffered corner often results for the Isolate Keep—or—Option.

To the slot side, a specialized quarterback Keep is used to take advantage of the favorable blocking angles which are usually gained from a wide slot alignment. The slot back is instructed to flex his position, then cut-block the defensive end while the split end carries out his shield block on the outside linebacker, rover back or inside safety.

To the tight side, a delayed option is used to take advantage of the slot back's timing in his swing-around into an option-pitch relationship. The Tight Side Option also has proven to be a stable sideline play, especially when run opposite a perimeter rotation. The tight end is instructed to slam the defensive end for a full count to falter his charge, and then release outside to force and block the defensive halfback into the sideline. A play-action quick pass is a good supplement to the Option.

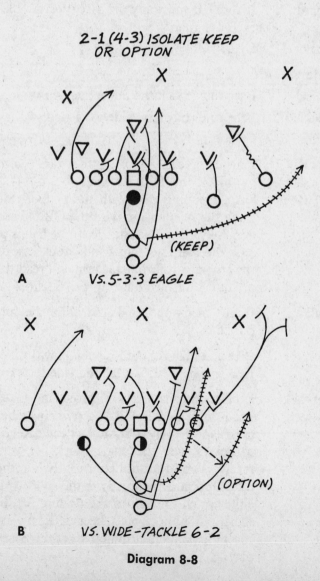

2-1 (4-3) ISOLATE KEEP OR OPTION

A   VS. 5-3-3 EAGLE

B   VS. WIDE-TACKLE 6-2

Diagram 8-8

ASSIGNMENTS:

Play-side

End	TE: slam DE for a full count, then release outside to force and block the DHB into the sideline (for option pitch). SE: shield block inside (for quarterback keeper).
Tackle	Ignore LB and apply the base rule (block inside vs. a 4-3 if covered by a LB).
Guard	Ignore LB and apply the base rule (double-team a 5-2 nose guard).
Center	Over; N/T, backside LB.

Backside

Guard	Base rule (block the down lineman vs. a Split-4).
Tackle	Base rule (block outside vs. a Split-4).
End	Crease.

Slot Back Play-side Keep—Adjust into a flex position and cut-block the DE! Backside Option—Leave on snap, stepping first with inside foot. Hurry to pitch the relationship with the QB, 4 yards deep and 2-3 yards to his outside. If the ball is pitched, look the ball into your hands, tuck it securely in the crook of your outside arm and read the block of your TE. Turn hard up the sideline!

Fullback Climb block the ILB and eliminate him from pursuit.

Tailback Give a full fake of the Isolation play. Influence the ILB and help block (gain outside leverage).

Quarterback Receive the snap, reverse pivot, and fake a deep hand-off to the TB. Give a convincing fake and do not rush the play. On the Slot Side Keep, sprint to get outside the angle blocks of your wide receivers and turn upfield quickly. On the Tight Side Option, run directly to the short corner and either pitch the ball to the trailing SB, or make sharp cut upfield on a keeper. Apply standard coaching pointers as indicated for the Base Option play.

COMMENTS: (Diagram 8-9) 21-22 TACKLE TRAP

The slot back Tackle Trap through the middle is a misdirection play that has the deceptiveness to break clean. This is due in part to (1) the concealed location of the slot back as an inside misdirection runner, (2) the advantageous timing of the tackle and the slot back hitting the trap hole a split second apart, (3) the running lane view of the slot back as he goes against the grain, and (4) the difficulty the defense has in making an early diagnosis (at the start, the play has similarities to a lead, isolation or power play, and even a quarterback set-up for a pass).

The Tackle Trap is delayed slightly in its development as compared to most guard-trap plays, yet the defense can be influenced out of position even further because of the backfield flow. With one of the larger athletes executing the trap block against a usually-large defensive tackle, an equalization factor exists. Also, this play helps to serve as a check measure against overzealous pursuit and acts as a deterrent to a crashing pass rush toward the slot side pass pocket.

ASSIGNMENTS:

Play-side

Tight End	Block acrossfield on the near safety.
Tight Tackle	Block near LB; if not applicable, block outside.
Tight Guard	Inside rule: unless the opponent is the target, then block outside.
Center	Block over. N/A, block backside.

Backside

Slot Guard	Base rule.
Slot Tackle	Pull from the line and trap behind the center (first opponent to show).
Split End	Crease.

Slot Back Align one extra step deeper than normal. On the snap of the ball, take the first step to the rear, but angle toward the inside. The next step squares the body laterally with the trapping tackle. Receive the ball with the inside elbow up, and follow the

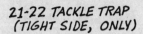

21-22 TACKLE TRAP
(TIGHT SIDE, ONLY)

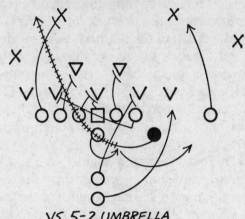

A   VS. 5-2 UMBRELLA

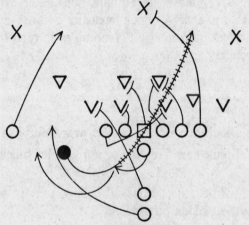

B   VS. SPLIT-4
    (SLOT BACK TAKES CONSERVATIVE FLEX)

Diagram 8-9

	trapping tackle, breaking behind his buttocks as the trap block is made.
Fullback	Drive outside the slot guard, fill the dive-hole and block.
Tailback	Swing toward SB, loop at DE and stop his charge.
Quarterback	Receive the snap, take a deep reverse pivot behind the dive hole, and make a forward hand-off to the

slot back as he clears through the middle trap lane. Continue around the end with a fake roll-out pass.

COMMENTS: (Diagram 8-10) 6-5 POWER

The Power slant is regarded as a ball-control play in the Slot-I structure as it is in most I-formation systems. Because of the tailback's opportunity to cut for daylight within the off-tackle area, it is considered a highly consistent play and reliable in all field positions. The Power slant is effective to both the tight and slot sides and can be adapted easily to a Power-I alignment.

Against some 8-man defensive fronts, such as a Split-4, the Power play is run best toward a wide (flex) slot. A wide slot usually will influence an 8-man front to slide a linebacker from an inside support position to an extended position to maintain its pass-coverage function in the flat. This adjustment should leave the defensive end positioned just outside the offensive tackle.

ASSIGNMENTS:

Play-side

End	TE: Block inside rule. N/T, block over (5-3 etc.). SE: Shield block inside; if wide slot, force DHB.
Tackle	Inside rule. If Split-4, may fold-block with the guard (optional).
Guard	Base rule, unless LB over—then apply inside rule.
Center	Base rule.

Backside

Guard	Base rule. Loop block a Split-4.
Tackle	Base rule: 3 counts, downfield. Loop block a Split-4.
End	Crease.
Slot Back	Play-side: Block inside. Flex into a wide slot against 8-man alignments, such as a Split-4, 5-3 etc., and block the OLB. Backside: Split crease (block #2).

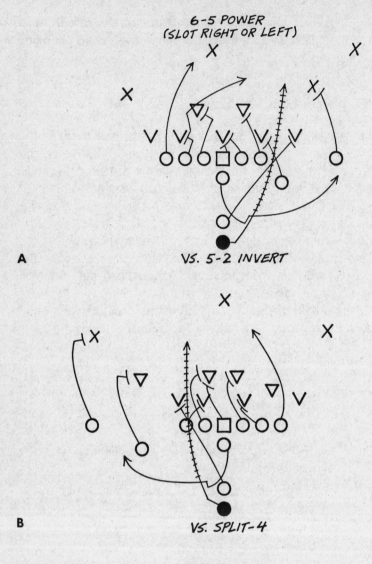

Diagram 8-10

Fullback   Take the first lead step sidewards and pointing
                     one yard deeper than the DE. The second step
                     parallels the first step to achieve a proper running
                     angle at a likely collision spot with DE. Adjust
                     course to accommodate the DE's behavior, then
                     climb block him and keep him tied up. Take the
                     DE in or out, wherever he wishes to go.

Tailback   Take the first step sidewards, but angling toward the off-tackle hole. The second step is made directly in line with the play hole. Get the inside elbow up for reception of the hand-off deep in the backfield. Look at the play-hole area after making the first step, and don't lose concentration, *Run at the hole and get all you can first, and look for daylight second.* If your body squares up properly after the second step, it is relatively easy to slide inside or outside at the point of attack: read the block of your FB.

Quarterback   Receive the snap, reverse pivot and hand-off the football as deep as possible in the backfield behind the tackle. Conceal your hands on your outside hip, and carry out a fake of a keeper around the corner.

COMMENTS: (Diagram 8-11) 16-15 LEAD OPTION

The Lead Option is a modified version of the "speed option" which evolved from the Split-T era. Its purpose is to give the defense an initial impression that a pass attempt is about to be made, thereby influencing its reaction, and then place option pressure at one of its corners with a lead blocker fortifying the pitch. The quarterback's intimidation of a pass gives him the needed depth in which to challenge the end, while it also draws the defensive line into a pass rush as its supporting linebackers make their pass-coverage retreat or press. The attack concept for the Lead Option, therefore, is to present a pass-read to the defense, then make it respond to a different kind of option pressure.

Like a speed option, a double-team block will usually take place inside the option point as both running backs swing immediately to their play-side corner. This allows the tailback to receive the option pitch in a position to turn up the sideline behind his fullback, the lead blocker, with the same explosive fury as gained from a power sweep or wishbone-type pitch-out. Note: we prefer to use the split end as a shield blocker when the Lead Option is run to his side, because this makes the play more secure in a short-yardage situation. Another play version, however, is to assign the split end to block the defensive halfback and let the fullback lead-block on the defender responsible for flat coverage.

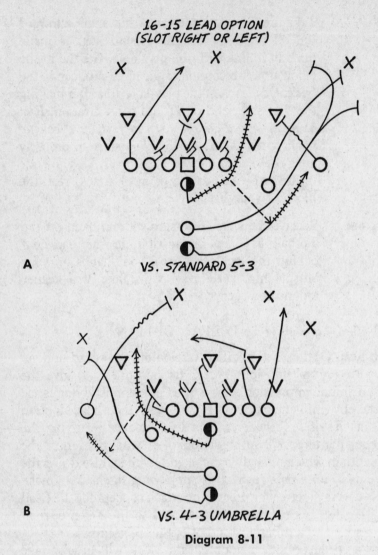

16-15 LEAD OPTION
(SLOT RIGHT OR LEFT)

A   VS. STANDARD 5-3

B   VS. 4-3 UMBRELLA

Diagram 8-11

ASSIGNMENTS:

Play-side

End	TE: block inside; N/T, block over.
	SE: shield block inside.
Tackle	Base rule; unless LB over, then block inside if applicable.
Guard	Base rule; consider a fold block with a tackle vs. a Split-4.

Center	Base rule.

Backside

Guard	Base rule.
Tackle	Base rule: 3 counts and release. Loop block a Split-4.
End	Crease.

Slot Back Play-side: block inside; if facing a Split-4 or 5-3 defense, flex into a wide alignment (if OLB is aligned deep, consider a switch-block with the SE and allow FB to area block at the wide corner). Backside: split crease (block # 2).

Fullback Step with onside foot, sprint to the play-side corner and lead-block on the DHB.

Tailback Take a drop step with the onside foot, to allow clearance from the FB, then swing into a pitch relationship with the QB 4 yards deep and 3 yards to his outside. Be prepared for an option pitch at all times, since quick pressure on the QB may necessitate an early flip-back. If the QB turns upfield, turn upfield with him and maintain a pitch relationship.

Quarterback Receive the snap, take an elongated skip backwards to achieve depth and land with both feet nearly parallel. Ball should be brought up at chest level as if setting up to throw in an attempt to false key the defensive read. Now, step with your onside foot and run directly at the inside shoulder of the DE to execute your keep or pitch option. Apply standard coaching pointers as indicated for the Base Option play.

COMMENTS: (Diagram 8-12) 8-7 SWEEP

The tailback Sweep is a consistent and productive wide play from the Slot-I formation because of its simplicity in blocking and quickness in reaching the outside. It is not a necessity, therefore, to devote extra time to its development, since it is not an intricate play to execute.

From a wide (flex) slot, the tailback Sweep has its best advantage when combined with a comprehensive passing attack. Corner adjustments of some form must be made by the opposing defense to cover the wide-receiver alignment, which, in turn, can give ideal blocking angles at the defensive corner. A widened split by the slot back can give him a desirable angle for a cut block on the defensive end, while his split end already has a favorable angle for a shield block on the nearside safety. This blocking advantage adds considerably to the reliability of the Sweep to the slot side of the formation.

As a tight side play, the Sweep from a Slot-I has its best advantage when run opposite a corner rotation of the perimeter. A considerable strain can be placed on the opponent's secondary at the weak corner when compensating measures are taken to cover the immediate pass-route release of the slot back and split end. Also, a tight side Sweep can have a damaging shock effect upon defensive linemen who attempt to slant-charge toward the slot side pass pocket.

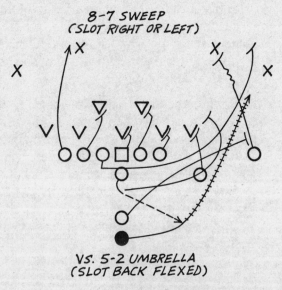

8-7 SWEEP
(SLOT RIGHT OR LEFT)

Vs. 5-2 UMBRELLA
(SLOT BACK FLEXED)

A

Diagram 8-12

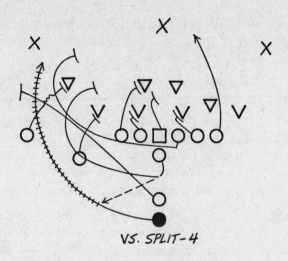

B   VS. SPLIT-4

Diagram 8-12 Continued

ASSIGNMENTS:

Play-side

End	TE: reach and hook block. SE: shield block (inside).
Tackle	Base rule.
Guard	Base rule.
Center	Base rule (check backside gap).

Backside

Guard	Pull from line behind the center and lead play around the corner.
Tackle	Fill for pulling guard. Loop a Split-4.
End	Crease.

Slot Back   Play-side: cut-block the DE. Backside: crease.

Fullback   Step with the close foot and sprint to the play-side corner. Your quick start is important in clearing for the pitched football, and in getting to the corner for the all-important kick-out block on the

DHB. If the DHB does not come up, go after him and seal him off to the inside.

Tailback   Step laterally with near foot, receive the pitch while "looking" the ball all the way into the hands, and turn the corner as quickly as possible. Speed is important in reaching the play-side corner. Read the block of your fullback and cut accordingly. When called to the tight side, run under control and read the defensive flow for a possible cut-back opportunity.

Quarterback   Receive the snap, reverse pivot, pitch the ball immediately with the near hand and swing wide to lead interference for your tailback. Your job is to wall off pursuit from the inside.

COMMENTS: (Diagram 8-13) 1-2 DRAW

The middle Draw play is one of the most elusive, yet most neglected, plays in high school football. Any team that uses the forward pass at a minimum of 20 percent of its playing time should include a draw play of some kind as a standard part of its offense. From the Slot-I, we like to set up the Draw from a pretense of a pull-up pass. The fullback, therefore, can be used to block the defensive end, as the tailback takes a long stride and an adjustment step to simulate a pass-protection block, and to ready himself for the football to be placed in his stomach at the exchange point behind the slot guard. The middle Draw should not be hurried, as the linebackers should be persuaded to read "pass," then retreat into their coverage zones while the defensive line is drawn into a hard pass rush. The quarterback is instructed to run in front of the waiting stance of the tailback and hand-off the football in a backward motion into the tailback's open arms. A rear hand-off exchange is made to allow room for the tailback's cutback run, without interfering with the normal course of the quarterback's setup behind the tackle. Once the hand-off is made, the tailback can explode into the uncovered hole at the tight side point of attack.

ASSIGNMENTS:

Interior Linemen   Each defensive lineman should be hooked away from the tight guard area with an aggressive pass protection block. If a blocker is covered by a LB, he should protect the inside rush lane for 2 counts, then go after his assigned LB within the short-pass coverage zone.

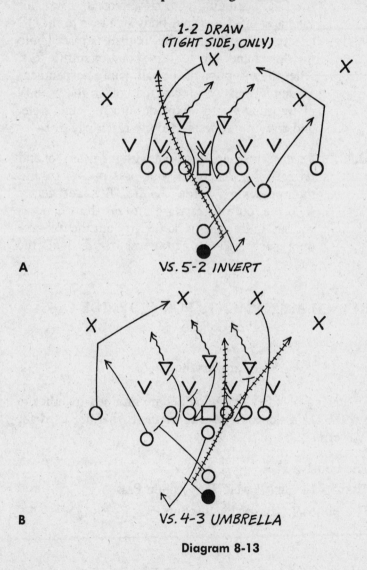

1-2 DRAW
(TIGHT SIDE, ONLY)

A   VS. 5-2 INVERT

B   VS. 4-3 UMBRELLA

Diagram 8-13

Tight End	Block acrossfield on the near safety.
Split End	Post route.
Slot Back	Scissor route (clear pass-coverage zone).

Fullback   Step with the near foot and climb-block the DE.

Tailback   Take a long stride and an adjustment step toward the DE, beginning with close foot, and wait for the hand-off. Keep your body sideways to the QB and remain still until the football is placed into the third hand. Do not lean, point or shuffle feet. After the reception of the ball, take a perpendicular step toward the uncovered hole in the vicinity of the tight guard. Explode into the open hole, and stretch out your stride to reach pay-dirt!

Quarterback   Receive the snap, front-out with the near foot and retreat immediately to your pass pocket behind the slot tackle (7 yards). As the TB is met, gently slide the football rearward into his third hand as you set up into the pocket. Carry out the full fake of a pass attempt and never "bird dog" the runner.

BACKFIELD ASSIGNMENTS FOR SLOT SIDE PASS PATTERNS

Standard Methods

The following backfield assignments are grouped together to cover the three basic slot side passing methods that are used for keystone patterns.

(1) The Pull-Up Pass
(2) The Off-Tackle "Power" Play-Action Pass
(3) The Fullback "Base" Play-Action Pass

Fullback:

(16-15 Pass) Climb block the first defender outside the slot tackle (ST), aiming at his inside shoulder to achieve an inside-out angle. If two defenders are outside the ST (Split-6, etc.), block the inside opponent and leave the outside opponent—the DE—to the TB.

(6-5 Power Pass)   Climb block the first defender past the ST.

(2-1 Base Pass)   Drive into the onside center-guard hole, give a convincing fake with the inside shoulder, plug the hole and block.

Tailback:

(16-15 Pass)   Climb block the outside defender—the DE. If double teaming with the FB on the DE, aim for the opponent's outside shoulder and put him on the ground. Never give enough air space inside for the defender to split the double-team block. Other blocking choices may include setting up inside your FB to check-block for internal leakage and also blocking to the backside.

(6-5 Power Pass)   Give full fake of the off-tackle Power play, and attempt to intimidate the defense into gang tackling. If not tackled, slide into the flat on a 5-yard Fan route, unless otherwise instructed.

(2-1 Base Pass)   Climb block the first defender outside your tackle.

Quarterback:

(16-15 Pass)   Sprint to the maximum depth in your pocket behind the ST. Set up quickly, square your shoulders and feet properly, scan your option selections, step at your target choice with the lead foot, and fire the football instantly on the time-beat.

(6-5 Power Pass)   Give a full fake of the off-tackle Power play, then set-up identically to the method used for a pull-up pass.

(2-1 Base Pass)   Give a quick jab fake to the FB, then set-up identically to the method used for a pull-up pass.

SUPPLEMENTAL METHODS

The following passing methods are offered as alternatives to the standard methods.

(1) The Sprint-Out Pass

(2) The Waggle Play-Action Pass to the Slot Side

(3) The Back-Pedal Pass

Fullback:

(18-17 Pass)	Climb block the first defender outside the ST. Attack his outside shoulder, maintain choppy steps, and rotate hips to outside. If two defenders are outside the ST (Split-6, etc.), block the inside opponent.
(18-17 Waggle Pass)	Drive through onside dive or off-tackle hole and fan into flat.
(Back-Pedal Pass)	Control ILB—either block area, buttonhook or flare as your linemen block inside-out on their rushers.

Tailback:

(18-17 Pass)	Climb block outside defender—the DE—at the play-side, attacking his outside shoulder. If the FB has same opponent, check his block, give aid as needed and clean-up the corner.
(18-17 Waggle Pass)	Fill block over the TG as he pulls from the line (plug hole).
Back-Pedal Pass)	Same assignment as FB (can mix blocking and outlet combinations).

Quarterback:

(18-17 Pass)	Sprint to a 6-yard depth and round the corner in a smooth turn, as shoulders square to the scrimmage line (necessary for run-pass execution). Mechanically it is natural to release the ball off the same foot as the passing arm (ie., right foot, right arm) and follow-through on the opposite foot—which is opposite that of a pocket pass. Sideline patterns should be stressed since the

	sprint-out pressure is on the corner and a running pass usually has a "heavy" nose-down trajectory.
(18-17 Waggle Pass)	Give a jab fake to the TB at the backside guard, reverse-around and take a rounding turn to acquire a 6-yard depth behind the ST. Square the shoulders to line, and exercise your choice to pass or run.
(Back-Pedal)	Push-off from line with right foot (if right-handed passer) and retreat backwards as rapidly as possible while facing the defense. Pull-up and release the pass on the time-beat of the pattern. A back-pedal pocket blends well with draws, screens, flares and buttonhooks.

A REVIEW OF PASS BLOCKING GUIDELINES FOR LINEMEN

Play-side Tackle and Guard:

Base rule (pop and pivot block, aggressively). If covered by a linebacker, check first for a blitz. If clear, the play-side tackle blocks the closest defensive lineman to appear, while the play-side guard blocks inside on the nose guard.

Center:

Base rule (get cut-off position). If covered by a linebacker, check for a blitz or inside slant. If N/T, cup block behind the line of scrimmage and seek out the defensive end.

Backside Guard and Tackle:

Cup protection (pop and pivot). If covered by a linebacker, check for a blitz and then drop backward to pick up the defensive end.

COMMENTS: (Diagram 8-14) FAN PATTERN

The Fan pattern is one of the most reliable, and probably the safest, of all traditional pass patterns because of the outside-leverage advantage that is usually gained by all receivers on their route break. The quarterback, therefore, is instructed to aim his pass between the sideline and his selected receiver, giving less chance of an interception from this type of pattern.

All of the fanning receivers are coached to take a sway inside before rounding to the outside—therefore the secondary is primarily attacked horizontally. The tight end fills into the underneath crease of the middle zone.

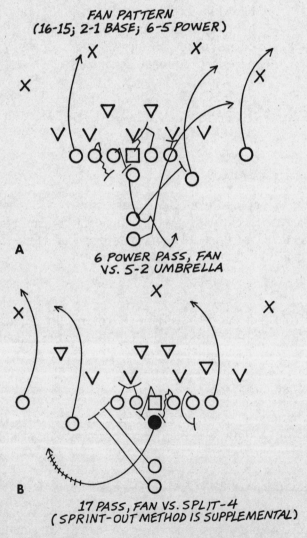

FAN PATTERN
(16-15; 2-1 BASE; 6-5 POWER)

A

6 POWER PASS, FAN
VS. 5-2 UMBRELLA

B

17 PASS, FAN VS. SPLIT-4
(SPRINT-OUT METHOD IS SUPPLEMENTAL)

Diagram 8-14

If a play-action Power Pass fake is used, the tailback can release into the flat at a 5-yard separation between each receiver from a 4-beat route break. This type of flood pattern, incidentally, is secure for a young and inexperienced quarterback.

RECEIVER ASSIGNMENTS:

Split End Fan route; break for the flag, looking outside (sway inside prior to the break).

Slot Back Fan route; level-off toward the sideline on the route break (sway inside prior to the break). Get behind an "inverted" defensive safety, if possible.

Tailback If the play-action fake of a Power Pass is called, drive off-tackle and make the defense commit itself. If untackled, release into the flat from a rounding curve, 5 yards at deepest point.

Tight End Middle crease.

COMMENTS: (Diagram 8-15) DIVIDE PATTERN

The Divide pattern is at its best against a strong-safety invert and rover (monster) type of secondary coverage. It is comparable to the Fan pattern in reliability and safety because of each receiver's advantage in achieving sideline leverage. The secondary is attacked vertically in the deep hole to the onside corner of the field by the slot back's Drive route, and it attacked horizontally in the flat by the split end's sideline break on an Out route. The tight end penetrates the middle crease, which helps keep the free safety occupied. This pattern combination places tremendous pressure on the perimeter decisions, which must be made at the coverage levels of the defensive corner.

Against an invert secondary, the split end is the normally open receiver. When facing a 4-deep umbrella coverage, the slot back is the prime receiver on his Drive route into the deep corner. The open receiver against a 3-deep rover secondary is dependent upon the coverage decision of the onside defensive halfback.

The Divide pass can be the core of a "two-minute offense." If a pass delivery appears unsafe, the ball can be thrown out of bounds easily on an early down when it is essential to stop the clock.

DIVIDE PATTERN
(16-15; 2-1 BASE; 6-5 POWER)

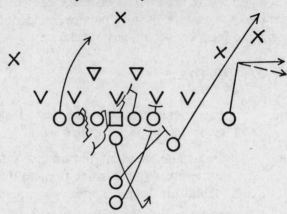

A   16 PASS, DIVIDE VS. 5-2 INVERT

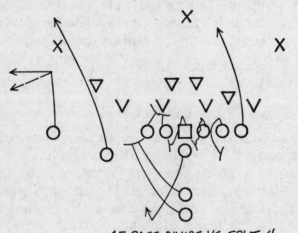

B   15 PASS, DIVIDE VS. SPLIT-4

Diagram 8-15

RECEIVER ASSIGNMENTS:

Split End   Out route (cut-off the inside foot at a controlled speed and breaks sharp toward near sideline). If crowded, angle slightly toward the line of scrimmage.

Slot Back   Drive route (go in a direct line at the corner—get outside leverage).

Tailback   Climb block or Fan (5 yards) on the Power Pass.

Tight End   Middle crease.

COMMENTS: (Diagram 8-16) SCISSOR PATTERN

The Scissor pattern is best used against an umbrella secondary, in which the defensive halfback (cornerback) can be confused when exposed to the quick pressure exerted in the onside flat, against a 3-deep zone-secondary. In this, the linebackers can be out-positioned in a foot race to the sideline. A pass release to the underneath receiver, the slot back, is technically safe and reliable in any field position.

The Scissor pattern stretches zone defenses in several ways. The slot back's Scissor route pressures the secondary, both horizontally and vertically, because of its slicing angle. The split end stretches the secondary vertically, after pressuring his defender with a fake of an Out-pass cut, before he breaks upfield on a Snake route. The tight end stretches the deep middle vertically on his Railroad route, which can be disastrous to a defensive safety who attempts to "fill" into the flat zone at the slot side, to cover the slot back's pass route.

The Snake route of the split end will either force a break-down at the deep outside, or it will help empty the flat zone for the slot back's Scissor entry.

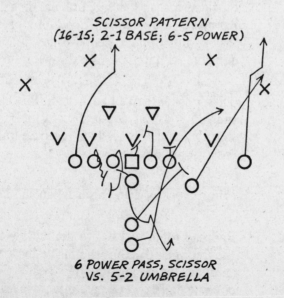

SCISSOR PATTERN
(16-15; 2-1 BASE; 6-5 POWER)

6 POWER PASS, SCISSOR
VS. 5-2 UMBRELLA

A

Diagram 8-16

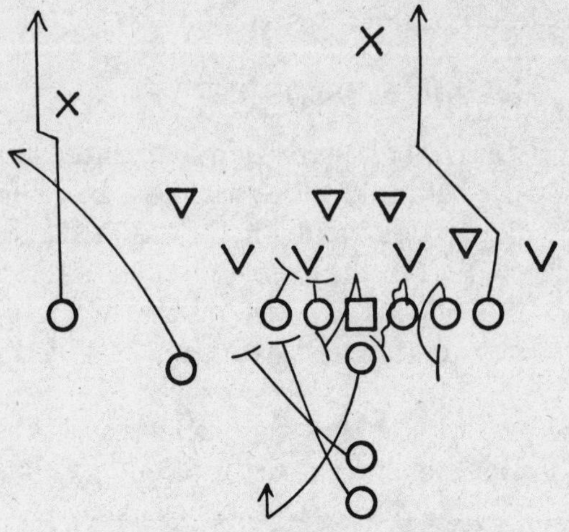

15 PASS, SCISSOR
VS. SPLIT-4

B

Diagram 8-16 Continued

RECEIVER ASSIGNMENTS:

Split End   Snake route (make the preliminary cut off of your inside foot on a brief Out pass cut, then plant the outside foot and break upfield in a full sprint parallel to the sideline). Look for a pass from the inside, but do not bend inside unless you are adjusting to the path of a thrown football.

Slot Back   Scissor route (drive in a straight line at an 8-yard spot on a 4-beat count directly over split end's starting point). Be ready to receive a quick-release pass from underneath.

Tailback   Climb block or Fan (5 yards) on the Power Pass.

Tight End   Railroad route (drive into the middle crease over the tight guard, plant the inside foot, then break straight upfield on the time-beat). Get into an opening and expect a pass directly over the center area.

COMMENTS: (Diagram 8-17) SCISSOR AND UP PATTERN

The Scissor and Up pattern was designed with the purpose of discouraging an inverted safety's tendency to crowd the slot back's Scissor-route release. By breaking the slot back deep after he enters the wide flat zone, the split end can execute an inside curl which can possibly open up two receivers, both of whom are in the quarterback's line of view.

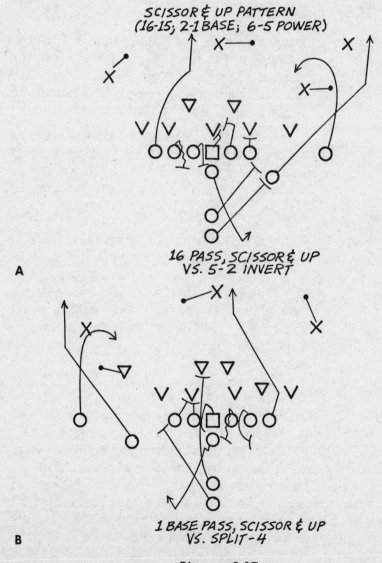

SCISSOR & UP PATTERN
(16-15; 2-1 BASE; 6-5 POWER)

16 PASS, SCISSOR & UP
VS. 5-2 INVERT

A

1 BASE PASS, SCISSOR & UP
VS. SPLIT-4

B

Diagram 8-17

The slot back should break upward from his Scissor route release at an approximate 8-yard depth (4-beat count) over the area of the split end's initial start. The split end takes his defender straight backward and breaks into his rounding turn inside at the depth of his time-beat. This combination gives a unique vertical stretch from the slot back and a crease-divider from underneath by the split end.

RECEIVER ASSIGNMENTS:

Split End   Inside Curl route (plant the outside foot at maximum depth, turn inside and square-up to the quarterback). Slide into any opening that can be found inside and stay there. Move laterally to adjust to the flight of the ball.

Slot Back   Scissor and Up route (drive in a straight line at an approximate 8-yard spot directly over the split end's starting point, and break up the sideline on a parallel course. Look for a pass from the inside.

Tailback   Climb block or Fan (5 yards) on the Power Pass.

Tight End   Railroad route (drive into the middle crease over the tight guard, then break straight upfield on the time-beat). Get into an opening and expect a pass directly over the center area. Take care not to run beyond this area, since this would result in a poor relationship with the quarterback and make a pass attempt futile.

COMMENTS: (Diagram 8-18) "X" PATTERN

The "X," pattern places extreme pressure on the secondary's deep middle, with an attempt to break it down vertically with a tight end and slot-back cross. The split end (second pass option) horizontally attacks the secondary with an Out break. A combination of two crossing receivers with a break-out wide receiver is an effective pass, both against zone and man-coverage secondaries. We favor a 4- and 5-beat count on this pattern, so that the crossing receivers can gain extra steps on the defenders assigned to them.

From a 5-beat release, the quarterback must feel that there is sufficient time to throw and that he has the "arm" to reach a deeper target. A 3-beat release will result in an early reception within the medium-range area over the center. With sufficient practice, the quarterback can learn to throw to a "spot" and let the intended receiver run to the football.

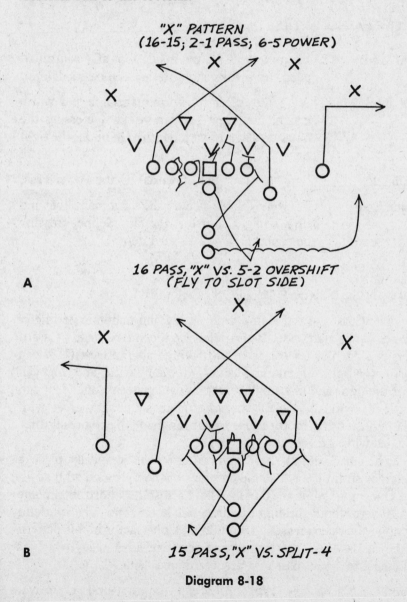

"X" PATTERN
(16-15; 2-1 PASS; 6-5 POWER)

16 PASS, "X" VS. 5-2 OVERSHIFT
(FLY TO SLOT SIDE)

A

B   15 PASS, "X" VS. SPLIT-4

Diagram 8-18

Quarterback Coaching Point: Experience has taught us that *all* patterns which involve a 2-receiver cross ("X," Cross, See-Saw, etc.) will take a longer secondary read than patterns without crossing receivers. Take this into account without holding the football too long.

RECEIVER ASSIGNMENTS:

Split End   Out route (cut off the inside foot at a controlled speed and breaks sharp toward the near sideline).

Slot Back   "X" route (clear the scrimmage line and run a straight course at the far sideline, crossing the center area at a 12-yard depth). Go under the tight end.

Tailback   Climb block or Fan (5 yards) on the Power Pass.

Tight End   "X" route (take a step off the scrimmage line, and run a straight course at the far sideline, crossing the center area at a 13-yard depth).

COMMENTS: (Diagram 8-19) CROSS PATTERN

The Cross pattern is important in helping maintain perimeter balance at the tight side. If the defensive secondary rotates toward the slot side, the offense is left with three alternatives: (1) it can explore the tight side running game—especially wide, and (2) it can favor the tight end as a single target on pass patterns, and (3) it can attack the weakside defensive corner at its vulnerable areas with crossing receivers. Preparations have been made to explore all three avenues with the Slot-I.

The idea behind the Cross pattern is to vertically place a backdoor strain upon a single coverage of the tight end with an In and Out route, while the crossing slot back splits a horizontal plane at a 10-yard depth through the tight side hook zone. The split end occupies the deep crease in the middle. A plus factor in this pattern is the across-the-grain timing and leverage advantage, which is beneficial to a lead pass at a predetermined "spot."

Quarterback Coaching Point: Although the first-option receiver group in this pattern is located at the tight side, a quarterback always must square-up to the scrimmage line and not point his lead foot at an intended target until the time of delivery. Strive to develop an instinct for an open receiver without losing poise.

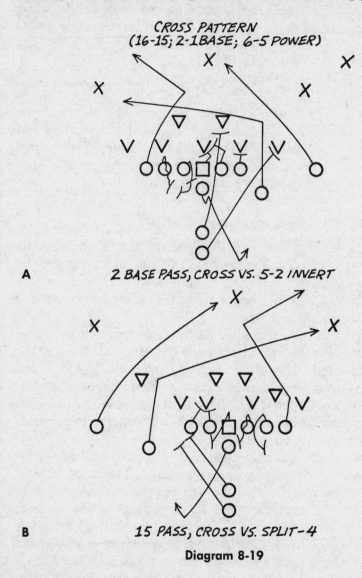

CROSS PATTERN
(16-15; 2-1BASE; 6-5 POWER)

A   2 BASE PASS, CROSS VS. 5-2 INVERT

B   15 PASS, CROSS VS. SPLIT-4

Diagram 8-19

RECEIVER ASSIGNMENTS:

Split End   Penetrate the crease deep over the center area (try to take at least two defenders with you). Look for a lead pass (raise your outside hand, *if* open).

Slot Back   Cross route (clear the line quickly with 2 or 3 steps, plant the outside foot and sprint to the far sideline at an angle, taking you to a 10 yard depth over the area of the tight end's initial stance). Use your all-out speed to reach the reception point. Look for a pass from underneath, between yourself and the sideline.

Tailback   Climb block or Fan (5 yards) on the Power Pass.

Tight End   In and Out route (drive into the middle crease over the tight guard, plant the inside foot and break hard for your onside corner). Try to pull your opponent inward, then break behind him, looking for a pass from the outside.

COMMENTS: (Diagram 8-20) SEE-SAW PATTERN

The See-Saw pattern is designed to confuse the deep-middle secondary defenders. As the slot back and split end sprint forward each makes a sharp break, the split end breaks to the deep middle (Post route), with the slot back cutting behind him, breaking into the deep corner (Flag route).

A vertical stretch is applied on the secondary defense by the crossing slot back and split end, while the tight end slips into the underneath middle-area at 6 yards on a Drag route. The tight end often opens up as the perimeter's safety is cleared from overhead. A complete secondary breakdown has been witnessed on occasions when defensive check-off communications failed, and two defenders were drawn into one zone.

A play-action pass fake (Base or Power) can be used to freeze the linebackers and help open up the tight end as an underneath receiver. A fake of the Power play will send the tailback out of the backfield on a course that splits the cross point. This, in effect, floods the deep onside third of the perimeter zone. The See-Saw pattern is sound against man-coverage secondaries also, since crossing receivers place a strain on this coverage. The flight of the football must have an adequate lead for a well-placed "spot" pass.

Quarterback Coaching Point: Slow receivers can make this pattern difficult to read. To help perceive a clean-break at the cross-point, the quarterback *can* instruct his slot side receivers to make their cut on a count sooner than the release of the time-beat.

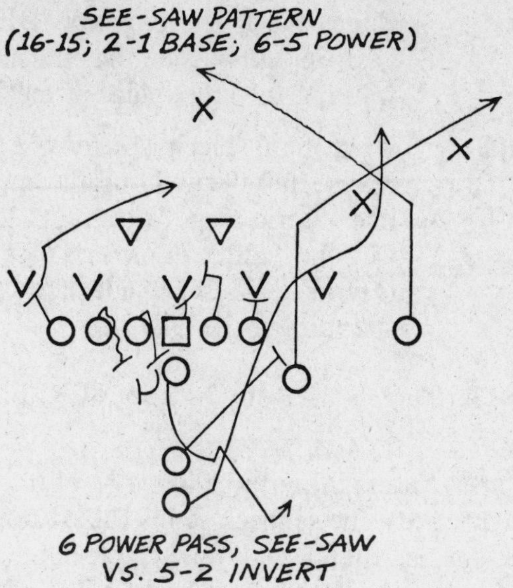

SEE-SAW PATTERN
(16-15; 2-1 BASE; 6-5 POWER)

6 POWER PASS, SEE-SAW
VS. 5-2 INVERT

A

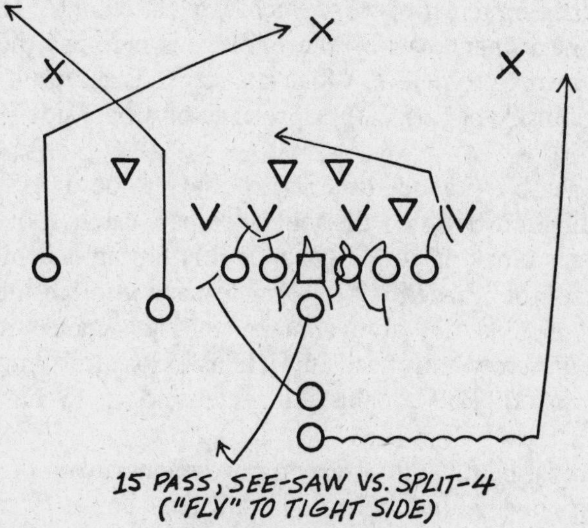

15 PASS, SEE-SAW VS. SPLIT-4
("FLY" TO TIGHT SIDE)

B

Diagram 8-20

RECEIVER ASSIGNMENTS:

Split End   Post route (cut to the inside off of the outside
                   foot). Get inside leverage.

Slot Back   Flag route (cut to the outside off of the inside
                   foot). Get outside leverage.

Tailback   Climb block the play-side DE. On the Power
                      Pass, release outside the end and *go up the chute,*
                      splitting the cross-point of the SB and SE.

Tight End   Drag route (block DE for one long count, then
                      release into the underneath zone 6 yards from the
                      line of scrimmage (distance of LB's coverage may
                      vary the depth). Look for a pass as the center area
                      is reached. Raise outside hand, *if* open, to get the
                      attention of the QB.

COMMENTS: (Diagram 8-21) 16-15 PASS, SCREEN RIGHT
(LEFT)

A Screen Pass to the tailback is a very reliable play to either the
slot or tight side. The tailback is instructed to go forward at his
play-side defensive end and false-block him. Then he circles
outward 5 yards and backward 2 yards, behind the forming wall of
offensive linemen to get his pass-catching position. This false-block
and circle-back maneuver by the tailback is hard for the rushing
defensive linemen to detect. When the screen is set up to the tight
side, the tailback begins with a pretense of a backside protection
block.

Considerable practice time is necessary to develop the necessary coordination between the tailback's pass catch and timing of
the linemen's blocking wall. But once this timing is achieved and
the linemen have learned not to allow leakage through their screen
wall, this play should always make yardage against a rushing
defense. The screen unit heads upfield as a close-knit human wall,
on the command "Ball", making the defense come to the wall—not
vice versa!

Care must be taken to prevent any defender from piercing the
wall or slipping behind it before the screen becomes organized.
This is why a full, 3-count release should be used, with the center
designated as a backdrift blocker.

SCREEN ASSIGNMENTS:

Playside

  End   Split End: Snake route (unless otherwise as-
                      signed). After taking defender deep, curl back

toward the sideline and seal off the inside. Tight End: force DHB (unless otherwise assigned). Stalk the defender and block him to the inside.

16-15 PASS, SCREEN RIGHT (LEFT)
(SLOT SIDE PULL-UP WITH
SCREEN WALL TO EITHER SIDE)

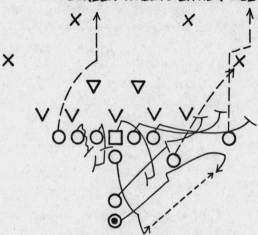

16 PASS, SCREEN RIGHT
(TO SLOT SIDE) VS. 5-2 UMBRELLA

A

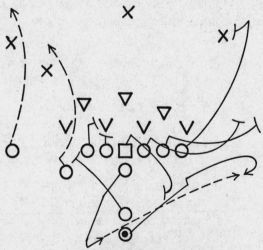

15 PASS, SCREEN RIGHT
(TO TIGHT SIDE) VS. 4-3 INVERT

B

Diagram 8-21

Tackle	Slam the near defender for 3 full counts; release to a set-up location 7 yards to the outside at the line of scrimmage. His responsibility is to defend an area from outside-in (block the DHB if he should advance up).
Guard	Slam the near defender for 3 full counts; release to a position inside the set-up of the ST. Establish a close relationship (4-5 feet) with the ST.
Center	Delay the near defender (base rule) for 3 full counts, then release to a location behind the original alignment of the ST or beyond. Pivot inside and look for any backside drift that may present a danger to the screen wall. On the command "Ball," release forward into the inner part of the wall where it is the most vulnerable to defensive penetration.

Backside

Guard	Cup protection (pop and pivot).
Tackle	Cup protection (pop and pivot).
End	Tight End: Railroad route (unless otherwise assigned). Seal off the inside. Split End: Snake route (unless otherwise assigned). Seal off the inside.

Slot Back Scissor route (unless otherwise assigned). Curl back toward the sideline and seal off the inside.

Fullback Climb block the first defender outside the tackle on the slot side for 2 full counts. As the screen wall is being set up to your side, join into the wall from the inside after releasing the defensive end.

Tailback Approach the DE as if attempting a climb block, then false-block him and circle back to a distance of 5 yards from the tackle and 2 yards behind the line of scrimmage. This ritual should end with the quarterback's release of the football. When the reception is made, yell "BALL" to the blockers in the screen wall, and follow behind them patiently.

Quarterback Receive the snap, front out with the near foot and pull-up on the fourth time-beat behind the ST.

Then fade back 2 more yards, pivot toward the lingering TB and throw a direct, but soft (lob), pass. A screen pass to an awayside receiver must carry more intensity in its delivery.

COMMENTS: (Diagram 8-22) 16-15 PASS, SCREEN MIDDLE

The Screen-Middle pass is used primarily in situations whenever the inside defense charges recklessly while the defensive ends take responsibility for outside containment. A screen up the middle can be a deterrent to blitzing tactics by inside linebackers, and it can be used to take advantage of linebackers who drop-off excessively into their hook zones in an overplay of their pass-play responsibility.

SCREEN-MIDDLE ASSIGNMENTS FOR INTERIOR LINEMEN:

1. All linemen from tackle to tackle bump-block their nearest defender, and allow each one to "fight through."
2. Next, the offensive line must release forward to a distance of 3 yards and wedge together tightly in a shoulder-to-shoulder relationship, with the offensive center as their apex.
3. When the runner yells "Ball," all linemen move forward in unison.
4. Inside penetration must not be allowed after the wall is formed, and the blocking unit must wedge through all obstacles.

RECEIVER AND BACKFIELD ASSIGNMENTS:

Tight End Go route, then stalk the defender and seal off the inside.

Slot Back Post route (block the near safety).

Split End Go route, then stalk the defender and seal off the inside.

Tailback Take 3 steps (beginning with the near foot) and circle back to the inside. Then set-up behind the center's original alignment (behind the line of scrimmage) and wait for the pass release from the

16-15 PASS, SCREEN MIDDLE

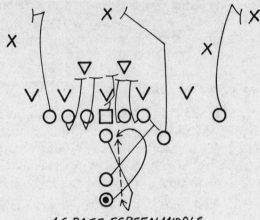

A

16 PASS, SCREEN MIDDLE
VS. 5-2 INVERT

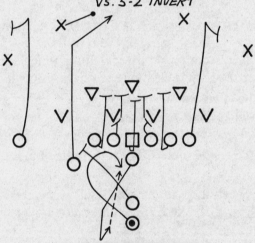

B

15 PASS SCREEN MIDDLE
VS. 4-3 UMBRELLA

Diagram 8-22

QB. "Look" the ball all the way into your hands. Yell, "Ball!" when the pass is caught, then turn and follow patiently behind the human wall up the middle.

Fullback   Climb block the first defender outside the tackle on the slot side.

Quarterback   Receive the snap, front out with the near foot and pull-up on the fourth time-beat behind the ST.

> Then fade back 2 more yards, pivot toward the center, and lob the ball to the waiting TB.

COMMENTS: (Diagram 8-23) QUICK PASS

The Quick Pass is an old stand-by from the Split-T era. Its use had faded somewhat in national popularity until the Veer-T helped revitalize it.

The Quick Pass should probably be used more often in all I-formation systems, since many defensive teams fail to fully honor their responsibility in the linebacker and corner zones when attempting to stop the strong rushing potential that an I-formation poses. This being the case, it is a simple matter for any of the up-front receivers to slip into these openings and take advantage of this easy-to-execute pass.

From the Slot-I, the split end runs a look-in approach into any obvious hole. The tight end and slot back have two basic choices—either straight-up, getting behind their defender, or arc inside, gaining inside leverage. In either case, the three receivers must jointly get the advantage, never running directly at a pass defender.

The Quick Pass is not classified in the stretching category, but instead is an exploitation of the zone creases in the short and mid-ranges. A well-timed Quick Pass can easily result in an instant score.

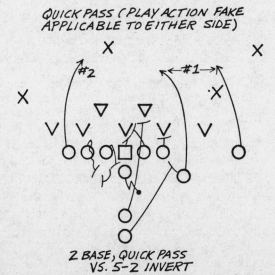

QUICK PASS (PLAY ACTION FAKE APPLICABLE TO EITHER SIDE)

#2   #1

Z BASE, QUICK PASS
VS. 5-2 INVERT

A

Diagram 8-23

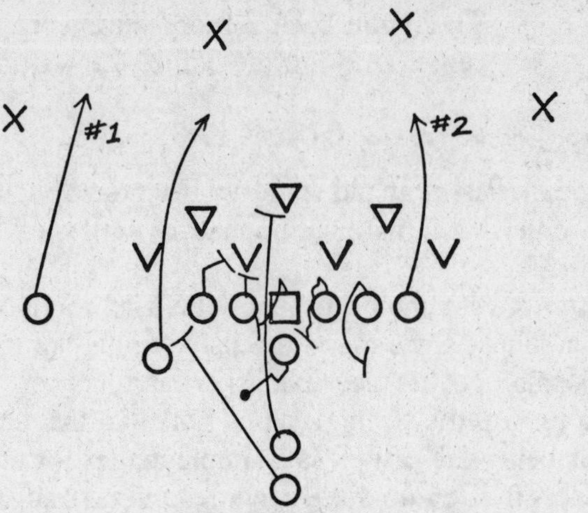

1 BASE, QUICK PASS
VS. 4-3 UMBRELLA

B

Diagram 8-23 Continued

RECEIVER AND BACKFIELD ASSIGNMENTS:

Split End   Hit the crease within the "curl" zone (take a look-in angle).

Slot Back   Hit the crease overhead or bend slightly inside.

Tight End   Hit the crease overhead or bend slightly inside.

Tailback   Climb block the first defender outside the offensive tackle to the side of the play fake.

Fullback   Drive into the assigned middle hole, giving a full fake of the Base play.

Quarterback   Receive the snap, front-out with a short step with the close foot, and fake a jab hand-off to the FB. Next, step back with a long stride and fire the ball to an onside receiver. If any linebackers present a danger, turn and look for a backside receiver. If no one is open, seek a running lane up the sideline.

COMMENTS: (Diagram 8-24) WAGGLE PASS, LEFT (RIGHT)

The Waggle Pass is the key play of the bootleg series. In spite of its simplicity, it is one of the most consistent passes in the offense. In fact, only a few special patterns have been added to expand and supplement our bootleg concept. The play's success largely depends upon the play-side linebacker becoming involved in the cross-action of the backs, so that the fullback will have an opportunity to slip through the line and gain a lateral advantage.

The tight end runs a Drive route into the deep corner, keeping outside leverage. The fullback goes through the dive hole or off-tackle, whichever has the least congestion, and then breaks into the flat on a simple Fan route. The middle crease is filled by the split end. The secondary is placed in a position to defend a vertical stretch on the tight side corner, plus a horizontal stretch underneath by the fanning fullback. The split end nullifies a secondary "roll" by piercing the deep middle.

A bootleg-action pass, in simple terms, is a quarterback roll-out which begins with a pivot after a play-fake is made. The quarterback's depth from the line, and his upper-body pass delivery remain fundamentally the same as from a pull-up. A distinction is made, however, in the quarterback's option choice to pass the football or to keep it and run for yardage. The pass receivers, consequently, should be given a time-beat on the 4th and 5th count, with the quarterback throwing on his own timing. From a supplemental split-back alignment, a fullback Waggle is practical to the slot side, if coordinated with a passing attack which is built around a cup-protection pocket.

ASSIGNMENTS:

Play-side

Tight End	Drive route (angle into the onside deep corner on a straight course, keeping outside leverage).
Tight Tackle	Base rule (pop and pivot block, aggressively). If covered by a LB, check blitz and then block the *closest* defensive lineman to appear.

WAGGLE PASS, LEFT (RIGHT)
(BOOTLEG TO TIGHT SIDE)

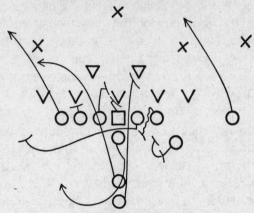

WAGGLE PASS, LEFT
A   VS. 5-2 COMBO COVERAGE

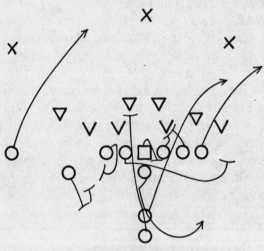

B   WAGGLE PASS, RIGHT
           VS. SPLIT-4

Diagram 8-24

Tight Guard	Base rule (pop and pivot block, aggressively). If covered by a LB, check blitz and then block inside on the NG.
Center	Base rule (get cut-off position). If covered by a LB, check for a blitz or an inside slant. If N/T, cup block behind line of scrimmage and seek out the DE.

Backside

Slot Guard — Step back with the inside foot, pull from the line behind the center, and take a cut-off path to meet the DE with a lead block at his farside jersey number.

Slot Tackle — Cup protection (pop and pivot). If covered by a LB, check for a blitz and then drop backward to pick up the nearest pass-rush threat.

Split End — Split the crease over the deep middle.

Slot Back

Cup protection (responsible for the DE). Protect the QB's back.

Fullback

Step with the near foot, drive through the dive hole or off-tackle, and then round-out on a 10-yard Fan route. Concentrate on gaining outside leverage on the LB.

Tailback

Fill over the SG as he pulls from the line. Allow no penetration.

Quarterback

Receive the snap, front-out step toward the slot side and give a quick jab to the TB as he fills over the guard. Then reverse-around without delay, taking a rounding turn at a maximum depth of six yards behind the TT, with shoulders squaring to the scrimmage line. Throw while on the run if a receiver is open, or pull-up and pass if the DE contains too deep. If all visible receivers are covered, or if there is an opportunity to take an obvious run, maintain a two-handed grip on the ball and turn upfield on a corner sprint.

REFERENCE NOTE: The blocking assignments that are applicable to the Waggle Pass should apply also to other additions used in the bootleg category.

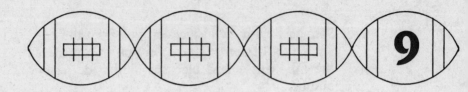

ENRICHMENT PLAYS

To supplement the keystone format, various enrichment plays have been included for use in special situations, and to strengthen a game plan against certain defenses. A special fullback sequence, as a format alternative, may also be developed around a fullback option series which incorporates sprint-out and play-action passing attacks. By interchanging some of the illustrated enrichment plays, a revised format could expand the role of the fullback with deceptive 3-way and trap options. A fullback option-series could retain the Base, Base Option, Quick Trap, Tackle Trap, Draw and Sweep plays, then add the Trap Option, Counter, inside Veer, outside Veer, Dive Option and Sprint Draw plays to complete the series (See Diagram 9-1). If the Quick Trap and Trap Option plays are emphasized heavily, the Dive Option should be given preference over the inside Veer. A 9-play format, in fact, consisting of the Base, Base Option, Quick Trap, Trap Option, Dive Option, Counter, Draw, Sprint Draw and Sweep plays could be used exclusively from a double-width alignment using two split ends and a flexed slot back. The deception of the sequence can be enhanced further by an intermingling of Quick passes to both sides of the formation, and by use of sprint-out and 18-17 waggle-action passes to the slot side. This offensive package is uniquely diversified and simple, and the personnel requirements for the series are basic to the Slot-I formation in that unlike a split-back veer attack, the inside and outside runners are specialized. This format alternative, which is our most current, has been adapted to a quarterback who can (1) run well, (2) execute the option's hand-off, keep or pitch decisions and, (3) throw reasonably well while on the run. A pocket-style passer who is a slow-footed runner may experience difficulty in running the options and in executing the sprint-out and bootleg passes.

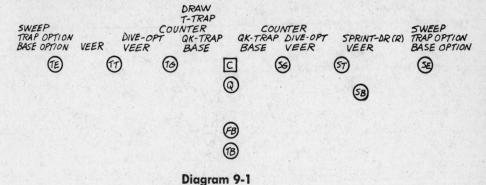

Diagram 9-1

A FORMAT ALTERNATIVE

New Plays for the Fullback Option Sequence

The Trap Option is a two-way keep-or-pitch option which goes hand-in-hand with the fullback Quick Trap (See Diagram 9-2). The Trap Option is probably the newest option innovation in modern football, and has gained rapid acceptance because of its deception and low-risk factor. The angle-blocking pattern of the Trap Option enables smaller linemen to compete against larger opposition, which is an attractive feature of the play. When the Trap Option was added to our attack, we found it best to have the backside guard trap the first down lineman to appear past the center, which is the target of the Tackle Trap play. This is instead of trapping the first defender to appear in the center-guard hole. The play-side tackle's assignment, therefore, is to block the near linebacker; if this is not applicable, he blocks outside. The play-side guard's rule is un-affected; he blocks inside, unless his opponent is the trap target; in this case he will block outside. The center is instructed to block backside if his nose guard is head-reading. He should double-team block the nose guard with his play-side guard, however, if the opponent is overly aggressive or if "shaded" over the play-side shoulder of the center. This revised trap rule should apply to the Quick Trap and the Trap Option, so that the two plays appear the same. Thereby, the burden of responsibility is placed upon the defender, who must contain the inside trap while trying to avoid being baited by the fullback fake when the option is run. The quarterback, after completing his backside fake and reverse-around turn, runs directly at the inside shoulder of the defensive end and executes the outside option (apply standard coaching pointers as indicated for the Base Option play).

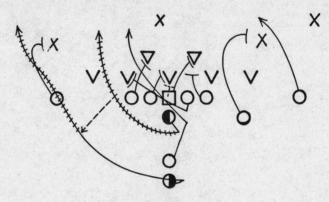

Diagram 9-2

The tailback Counter provides a straight-blocking alternative for the Cross Trap play, with near-identical backfield action (See Diagram 9-3). Since the frontside blocking pattern of the Cross Trap closely resembles the inside Veer, the revised Quick Trap and the Trap Option, a guard-trap is not practical for a tailback misdirection play within the play format of the fullback option sequence. This is because of the heavy reliance already placed upon the tackle's inside-rule blocking. The Counter play begins with the quarterback faking a quick-opener to his fullback through the backside center-guard gap; then he reverse pivots away from the scrimmage line to make the ball exchange to his tailback. The tailback, after taking a delayed counter-step behind his fullback, sprints for the inside leg of the farside guard to receive his hand-off and scan for an opening either inside or outside the guard. The base-blocking rules for the 1 and 2 holes will cover all traditional defensive situations effectively, including the four-against-three ratio that is characteristic of Split-4 alignments.

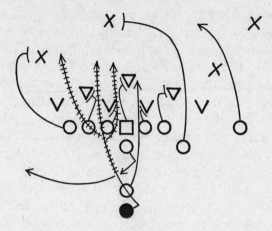

Diagram 9-3

The Veer option imposes a 3-way threat of an inside hand-off, off-tackle keep or wide pitch. The Slot-I is well-suited for the Veer option, since its play assignments already are specialized for the fullback, tailback, tight-end or slot back and split end positions (See Diagram 9-4). The option begins with the fullback blasting through the play-side guard-tackle seam, while the quarterback executes his ball ride with the fullback as in the Base Option, but in this case it occurs a step wider. It is important for the fullback to place a soft arm-fold over the football during the ride phase and to never tug at the ball when the quarterback decides to withdraw it during his initial read. The running lane for the fullback is walled-off by the block of the play-side tackle, whose assignment is to block inside and seal-off the area over the guard. When the Veer option is run to the slot side, the slot back and split end can be assigned either to switch-block or to force the onside half of the perimeter, leaving two defenders (usually) unblocked at the scrimmage line. When the play is run to the tight side, the tight end is assigned to slam the defensive end, to break his charge, and then release outside to force and block the defensive halfback into the near sideline. The unblocked opponent outside the play-side tackle becomes the read key for the inside hand-off; the outside defender is considered an option key. The quarterback is instructed to initiate his hand-off, unless the read key pinches inside to take the fullback dive. The hand-off read is given first priority because a failure to recognize the hand-off read is the most common mistake made by high school quarterbacks on triple option plays. When the quarterback reads a "keep," the ball is withdrawn from the fullback's belt-buckle area *before* the quarterback's arm flow can extend forward. His option course must remain along the scrimmage line, attacking the inside shoulder of the outside defender for execution of the keep-or-pitch option (apply the standardized coaching pointers of the outside-option technique). In Chapter 10, a broader explanation of our blocking assignments for the Veer Option will be given.

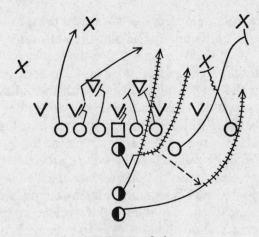

Diagram 9-4

The 5-6 Veer is an outside veer option, which develops one hole wider than the 3-4 Veer (See Diagram 9-5). The running crease for the fullback is established off-tackle: the starting point for the quarterback's 3-way option read. The fullback's drive for the off-tackle hole begins with a bending course similar to the 5-6 Trap, but is aimed for the outside leg of his play-side tackle. The running lane is walled-off by the inside block of the play-side tight end or slot back, whose assignment is to seal-off the area over tackle. The unblocked opponent located outside the tackle, usually a defensive end, is considered the quarterback's read key which determines his hand-off or keep segment of the option. The footwork of the quarterback starts with a near-parallel front-out step before meeting with his fullback on the third step, at a junction point located a yard behind the line of scrimmage. The fundamental execution of the ball ride and hand-off read are very similar to the 3-4 Veer. As a reminder, the quarterback should read "give" unless his read key (defensive end) pinches inside. If the read key is feathering, or if there is some doubt about his intentions, a hand-off should be made. When a "keep" is read, however, the quarterback should withdraw the ball from the fullback's belly and then turn upfield. Before executing an option pitch to the tailback, the quarterback should attempt to flatten the pursuit angle of his option key (rover back, strong safety or defensive halfback). The tailback must achieve width quickly for the pitch, which is not a difficult task from an I-back position.

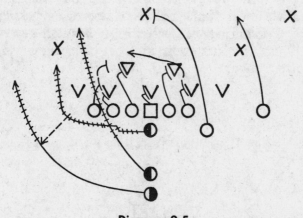

Diagram 9-5

The Dive Option is a zone (base) blocking version of the inside Veer play, with provisions made to pick up defensive stunts and slants (See Diagram 9-6). The quarterback's read for the 3-way option, and the assignments for the backfield and receivers are identical to the inside Veer. The Dive Option can be run equally well against reading and slanting defensive fronts, and is a natural complement to the Quick Trap and Trap Option combination. Base-rule blocking is used at the onset by all interior linemen, as each blocker takes an area step toward the pitch side before driving upward to make contact with his assigned defender. The purpose of the play-side tackle's area (reach) step is to make an attempt to establish inside-shoulder blocking contact with the outside shoulder of the read-key, and thereby influence a head-read and subsequent widening of the guard-tackle hand-off seam. If the read-key should hang, however, the tackle maintains blocking leverage for the outside option. If the read-key should close inside, the tackle then is free to arc for the inside linebacker and wall him off from the quarterback. The purpose of the area (scoop) step by the blockers located inside the hand-off lane is to protect the internal gaps from penetration, and also to add flexibility to the play's blocking design by providing a systematic means of picking up angle charges from the defensive linemen. Whenever a defensive slant occurs, the backside tackle, guard, center and play-side guards are responsible first for scoop-stepping underneath any defensive charge or stunt directed at their assigned gap, whether these originate from a head-up or from an adjacent defensive position. Their second responsibility is to pick up a linebacker from the backside, if left uncovered when a slant materializes. These zone-blocking innovations take place during the quarterback's hand-off read. Refer to Chapter 10 for a broader explanation of our blocking assignments for the Dive Option.

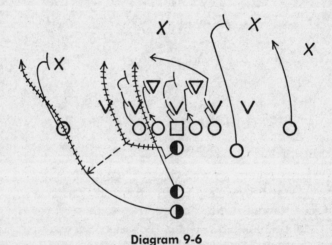

Diagram 9-6

The tailback Sprint-Draw complements a sprint-out passing attack and fortifies the Slot-I offense with an excellent off-tackle replacement play when the slot back is flexed into a wide alignment. This play is advantageous, especially to a talented "soft spot" runner who can capitalize upon the pass-read retreat of the linebackers. Pass blocking guidelines are applied along the scrimmage line, with the exception of (1) a backside assignment for the center, tight guard or tight tackle, who is uncovered to show pass, protect first against a blitz, then pull behind the covered lineman to the play-side and lead-through on the onside linebacker, and (2) a play-side assignment for the slot tackle and slot guard to fold-block against a stacked interior such as a Split-4 defense. A deep hand-off exchange behind the tackle should be made to the tailback on his third step, as he simulates a pass-block approach toward the onside end. The tailback should remain sideward to the quarterback and ready his arms for the placement of the ball as the quarterback makes his forward hand-off, then clears from behind on a sprint-out running course (See Diagram 9-7). A play-action pass fake of the Sprint Draw, incidentally, can be substituted easily for the pass fake of the Power play.

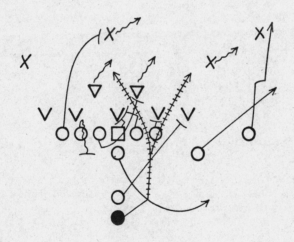

Diagram 9-7

OTHER ENRICHMENT PLAYS

The tailback Lead play is used to penetrate the play-side guard-tackle hole with a security blocker—the fullback—serving in a clean-up capacity. The Lead play, in effect, is a form of isolation play with straight, base-rule blocking. Its effectiveness will depend, naturally, upon the type of defensive alignment that is faced. It is especially useful against a middle bubble defense, such as an eagled 4-3, and against a floating linebacker defense (See Diagram 9-8).

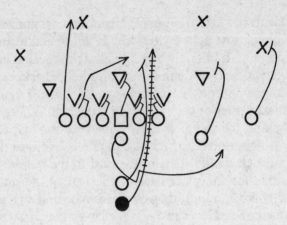

Diagram 9-8

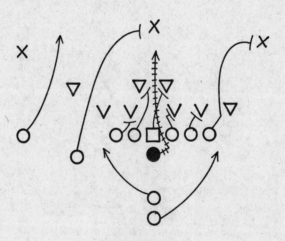

Diagram 9-9

The Goose play is our name for a quarterback sneak. This is a necessary play for short-yardage and goal line situations, and also is a ready "automatic" for the quarterback at any time the defensive middle is vacated. As an automatic, the quarterback darts up the middle on the designated snap count while his teammates unknowingly run their play assignments. As a predetermined call, the play is executed on a silent count which is triggered by the quarterback's hands rising up into a ball-snap position under the center. When the offensive linemen hear the sound of the ball snapping into their quarterback's hands, each blocker fires across the scrimmage line and makes immediate contact with his assigned opponent, while the I-backs scatter to mis-key the linebackers. Against an 8-man front with base blocking, a 2-hole blocking rule should be applied (See Diagram 9-9). Wedge blocking may be included as well.

The Tackle Trap Pass is an extension of the misdirection action from the 21-22 Tackle Trap play. Success with the running play helps to isolate the opponent's coverage of receivers, giving cred-itability to its companion play-action pass. The backfield pattern of both the run and the pass are identical, so efficient use is made of the fullback's course through the dive hole when he becomes a potential receiver on the pass call (See Diagram 9-10). As the slot back completes his running-play fake, he reinforces the backside protection while the tailback arcs at the defensive end to execute his climb block. After completing a fake hand-off to the slot back, the quarterback rolls-out toward the near sideline and releases his pass on a precalled 4th or 5th time beat. The pass coverage of the perimeter is stretched horizontally by the split end and fullback as they break on their Fan routes. The tight end splits the crease over the deep middle and seeks an opening beyond the center. Note that the quarterback's fake-and-roll technique resembles the waggle-action method; therefore, the Tackle Trap Pass could blend easily into the overall scheme of the aforementioned option sequence.

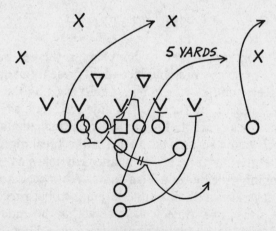

Diagram 9-10

The Divide Pass Left or Right is a continuation of the tight side bootleg pass concept, and therefore, is designated by direction, not by pocket number. Like the Waggle Pass Left or Right, it is used to take advantage of a perimeter's single coverage on the tight end. Since the Divide pattern is familiar to the slot side attack, its occasional use at the tight side presents no problem. The tight end's route stretches the secondary coverage horizontally with his sideline break on an Out route, while the fullback stretches it vertically in the deep hole to the onside corner of the field. Covering a receiver out of the backfield on a deep route can cause confusion in the perimeter decisions of the opponent. The mechanical function and play assignments of this and other bootleg passes are basically the same (See Diagram 9-11).

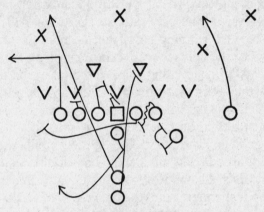

Diagram 9-11

SEE PATTERN

The See pattern is used to complement the See-Saw pass. It can be called upon any time the secondary presents an obvious hole within its deep middle or deep outside. By starting the pattern off on a forward release by the two slot side receivers, the secondary defenders are jockeyed into holding their original alignment. Then the slot back takes an outside hitch, before breaking inside on a Post route while the split end simultaneously takes an inside hitch before breaking outside on a Flag route. A vertical stretch of the secondary coverage gives favorable leverage to both receivers. The tight end is placed in a strategic location within the underneath part of the deep-middle, by his delayed release on a Drag route. Note that a fake of the Power play will send the tailback out of the backfield, on a course that splits the receiver's separation point which, in effect, floods the deep outside third of the perimeter (See Diagram 9-12).

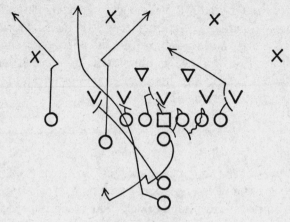

Diagram 9-12

TRAIL PATTERN

The Trail pattern is a favorite in testing the theory of the vertical-stretch. The pattern begins with the slot back taking his onside safety as deeply as he possibly can on a Go route. At this time, the split end is releasing off the line on a straight, deliberate, take-off for 5 steps (4 from his left). He then plants his outside foot, nonchalantly cuts inside and "trails" directly behind the path of the outgoing slot back. An emptying of the deep middle zone now takes place from the forcing tactic of the slot back, which creates a void underneath. This void can be slipped into by the trailing split end.

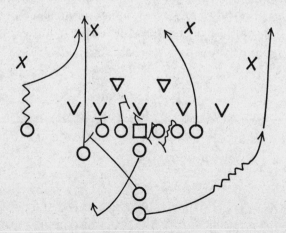

Diagram 9-13

If the safety should linger, the slot back may be the open receiver on his Go route. Therefore, the quarterback is instructed to read the perimeter coverage and throw to either of the receiver choices, since both are in his line of view. As illustrated, a Flare or Flare-and-Up route by the tailback can be included in this pattern and in many of the others (See Diagram 9-13).

CLOSING ANALYSIS

The twelve running plays and pass patterns that have been prescribed for the keystone offense and its alternatives, will give a relatively simple and rounded attack. The recommended plays and patterns are those which have survived a process of trial-and-error over a period of years.

Experience has made it evident that the fullback should always play a major role in the basic attack. A past trend of many I-formation systems has been to use the tailback in a running capacity 90 percent of the time. But this practice may have been short-sighted. With the fullback having such an access to hitting the line of scrimmage quickly, surely it is a waste not to make use of him as a functional runner.

If certain skills are lacking at one or more positions, the keystone format should be wrinkled or varied to adjust to a deficit in a given situation. Interchangeable resources are available, in the contents of this book, to broaden the application of the Slot-I's format. It is suggested, however, that adjustments in the keystone structure be decided only from the findings gained through your scrimmage experience. And, while a special play or two can be included for any upcoming game, it would be unwise to exceed a dozen plays and patterns as the basic offense.

ANALYSIS OF KEYSTONE PLAY BALANCE

Distribution		Area		Direction	
Tailback plays	5	Wide	4	Flow side	8
Fullback plays	3	Off-tackle	2	Misdirection	4
Slot back plays	1	Inside	6	(Total)	12
Option plays	3	(Total)	12		
(Total)	12			(Blocking Categories)	
		Formation		Straight	4
		Mirror plays	9	Trap	4
		Specialized	3	Combination	4
		(Total)	12	(Total)	12

Pass Pattern Concentration		Identification
Sideline at Slot Side	5	Fan, Scissor, Scissor and Up; Divide, Screen.
Middle zone	4	Quick, See-Saw, "X", Screen Middle.
Sideline at Tight Side	3	Cross, Waggle, Screen.

*The area of pass reception will vary with the choice of receiver, and his location during the timed release of the pass.

Table 9-1

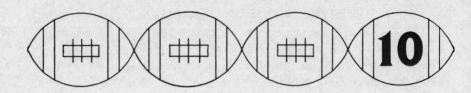

BLENDING THE VEER
WITH THE SLOT-I

A practical supplement to the Slot-I attack is a Slot-Veer alignment, with its split backs positioned directly behind the offensive guards. The most significant contribution of this twin-dive alignment to an I-back offense is the quarterback's opportunity to execute a straight hand-off on a forward plane, that is within the proximity of the attack hole. Since most I-back hand-offs are approximately 3 yards deep to the tailback and a step or two off the scrimmage line to the fullback, a raised-level exchange zone—termed a "mesh point"—can be utilized from a veer alignment to add yet another response situation for the defense. This instant-hand-off threat places tremendous pressure on the defensive front wall, especially when the guard-tackle dive play is complemented sufficiently with keep-or-pitch options and quick counters along the line of scrimmage.

Most of the play format of the Slot-I can be interchanged with a Slot-Veer, making it easy to blend the two systems together. But due to a loss of centralized running angles for the two running backs in a veer alignment, we prefer not to run isolation, lead or power plays, which are strong features of an "I," because they are not well-suited to this alignment. It is our philosphy that a play-fake intimidation should take place prior to any hand-off to an awayside halfback. This is a principle carried over from the popular Georgia Tech Belly-T of the 1950s.

Before you consider blending a veer backfield with the Slot-I, first analyze the availablity of an athlete at quarterback who possesses the necessary aptitude, confidence and reflexes to handle the various option plays. After all, if all the wrong decisions are made by the quarterback, or if he mishandles the essential mechanics of the options, the talents and efforts of the other ten athletes will be wasted. The success of a veer series depends upon the quarterback's ability to make the correct decisions and execute its functions, for it is he who must manipulate the option plays and make them work successfully.

We began to experiment with a veer alignment during the senior year of the outstanding quarterback Alan Risher, whose career credentials include two All-State Most Valuable Player honors, plus first-team berths on the Parade Magazine and Adidas (Scholastic Coach magazine) All-American Teams. At that time, the veer addition helped to control the opposition's strong pass rush by placing special emphasis upon veer and dive options, the trap plays of the keystone attack, and also, the draw plays, the flare and the screen passes that were modified for a back-pedal pass pocket.

ALIGNMENT ORGANIZATION AND SPACING

The Slot-Veer alignment is adapted to a style of offense designed for option plays and a pro-type passing attack. With an emphasis on options and cup-protection passes, it is best to split both ends so that the corner support of the defensive perimeter can be loosened at each side. From a double-width arrangement of the two ends, the slot back should take his maximum split of four yards to the wide side of the field to extend the perimeter's short-corner coverage, and also to improve blocking leverage when forcing and sealing off an outside linebacker, rover-back or onside safety. (Diagram 10-1.)

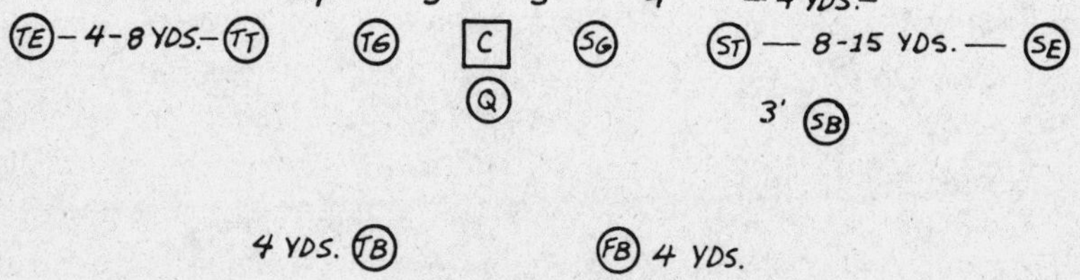

Diagram 10-1

In the Slot-Veer set-up, it is very important that the guards maintain a constant, 3-foot split from the center, and the tackles maintain a constant, 4-foot split from the guards. Exactness in spacing, blocking position and running angle are vital requirements for a veer option series to succeed. It is recommended that the Slot-I's flip-flop concept be retained, with the fullback always aligned on the slot side and the tailback always aligned on the tight side.

The placement of the slot back to the right or left in the formation should depend upon several factors. Normally, the slot back should declare (1) to the wide-field side, for the purpose of serving as a lead blocker in front of an option pitch where breakaway runs are most likely to occur, (2) to the play-side of an option call, when facing a balanced, 8-man front with outside linebackers such as found in a Split-4 and 5-3 defense, (3) to the short-field side, when a perimeter rotation can give the option advantage to the formation's open side, and (4) to the short-field side also, when there is a lack of defensive support at the sideline, which then gives the slot back an opportunity to use his needed minimum spacing for off-tackle play blocking.

COMPARATIVE PLAY CHART

In the chart below, the play format of the Slot-I is matched with a prescribed format for the Slot-Veer alignment. As previously stated, most of the Slot-I's keystone offense can be carried over to a veer backfield. For those plays that are not suited for a split-back set, substitutions have been made that will enhance this alignment.

SLOT-I	SLOT-VEER
1-2 Draw	Same (with modifications)
1-2 Quick Trap	Same
21-22 Tackle Trap	Same
1-2 Base	Same
1-2 Base Option	3-4 Dive (or X) Option
1-2 (3-4) Isolate	1-2 Counter Dive
1-2 (3-4) Isolate Keep—or— Option	1-2 Counter Option
3-4 Cross Trap	Same
15-16 Lead Option	Same
5-6 Trap	Same
5-6 Power	3-4 Veer
7-8 Sweep	Same

Table 10-1

FORMAT SUBSTITUTIONS

The Veer play replaces the off-tackle Power play from the Slot-I. In our version of the triple-option's original blocking scheme, the play-side tackle blocks inside on the near lineman or linebacker, while the play-side guard either blocks base or inside, whichever gives the best blocking leverage or double-team advantage (See Diagram 10-2). The block of the play-side guard should be flexible in coping with gap and stack situations and in physically handling tough interior linemen. With base blocking used elsewhere along the line, the two outside defenders at the play-side now are left free for the quarterback's inside and outside read on his 3-way option.

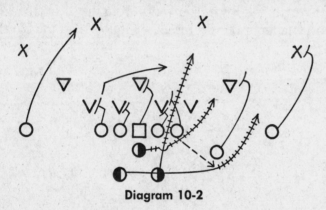

Diagram 10-2

Simplicity is given to the option mechanics of the play by making use of a contemporary read technique at the play-side dive hole, which is reasonably fail-safe and eliminates much of the high-risk factor. The following coaching points apply to the execution of the Veer play with its inside-crease blocking pattern:

1. *Dive man:* Drive on a straight approach into middle of dive hole and run through the football. If the football remains suspended for the hand-off, clasp over it with both arms and continue churning on an outside-angle sprint. Note: the running-lane approach of the dive man always must be the same and he should never bend inside on an option "give."

2. *Quarterback:* Step forward into the line and point the football directly at read key, the number two man from outside. Intimidate the read key as if to say "take the ball!" If the read key hangs in place or steps straight across line of scrimmage, leave the ball for exchange with the dive man.

Then continue down the line on a fake of an outside option, to prevent a collapse on the inside hand-off. If read key commits inside during the inside read, however, *withdraw* the ball a split-second before arrival of dive man, continue down the line and attack the inside shoulder of the outside defender, to execute a keep-or-pitch option (apply standardized coaching pointers of the outside option technique from the Slot-I). Note: the quarterback *never* inserts the ball when he reads "keep!" This virtually eliminates a fumble risk, a delay in timing or indecisiveness within the exchange zone.

3. *Pitch man:*Swing into an option-pitch relationship of 4 yards in depth and 3 yards in width from the quarterback (same orientation given for the Base Option from the Slot-I).

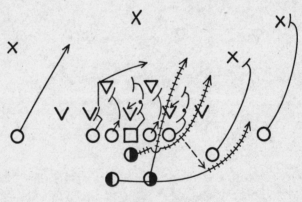

Diagram 10-3

The Dive Option replaces the Base Option play from the Slot-I. Its function is to use zone blocking principles for the 3-way option (See Diagram 10-3). Although the Dive Option takes the form of a base-block option, accomodations are made to pick up defensive slants without a loss of blocking contact on the read-key defender. The concept of zone blocking gained national prominence when defensive alignments began to disrupt the quarterback's hand-off read with their redesigned line slants and refined "shadow" techniques. These techniques crowded the offensive tackle's inside block and thereby freed their loose-playing linebacker to "scrape" the off-tackle lane. As a deterrent to these defensive tactics, the Dive Option first assigns its backside guard, center, play-side guard and play-side tackle to take an area step to the pitch side and then to carry out their base assignments, or to pick up their back-up assignment, in case of a line slant opposite the play flow. An area step by the play-side tackle also tends to widen the running lane for the option's inside hand-off against a head-reading opponent. The following application of zone-blocking techniques applies specifically to the Dive Option play:

1. *Backside guard:* Scoop step at the onside gap and look for a slant from inside. If none appears, block by the base rule (man over).

2. *Center:* Scoop step at the onside gap and use a cut-off block to protect against penetration from either direction; if a direct gap charge does not appear, square-up and block base (man over).

3. *Play-side guard:* Step across the outside gap and look for a slant from the read key. If he slants, cut-off block with the inside shoulder; if he hangs, square-up and block by the base rule (run up through the face of 5-2 linebacker). Note: against a Split-4, Eagle 5-2 or 4-3 defense, take a scoop step at the outside gap and block the near defender (base rule) to prevent penetration through the guard-tackle gap.

4. *Play-side tackle:* Step for the outside shoulder of the read key, attempting to widen him and soften his charge at the scrimmage line. If he should close inside, go immediately for the inside linebacker. Note: against a Split-4, drive immediately for the inside linebacker (base rule). If the read key is an outside linebacker (Eagle 5-2 or 4-3), maintain contact on the outside shoulder.

A cross-blocking alternative at the play-side guard-tackle hole can be a useful change-up in placing added pressure on the read-key opponent. Termed as the X-Option, the quarterback's inside read is unchanged with this X-block wrinkle (Refer to Diagram 10-4).

Coaching Point: if the read-key's reaction to the dive man is unclear to the quarterback, it may be helpful to go with the inside hand-off during the first few dry runs, and then carry out the outside option after an inside punch has been established.

The Counter Dive replaces the Isolate play from the Slot-I. It is one of the simplest and easiest ways to test a defensive over-reaction

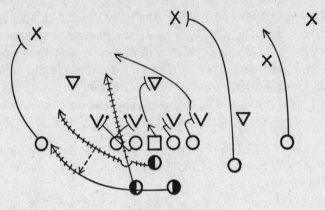

Diagram 10-4

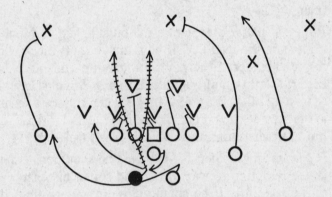

Diagram 10-5

to frontside hand-offs which occur on Base, Veer and Dive (or X) Option plays. With its origin dating back to the Split-T era, the Counter Dive remains a key play in the majority of option-oriented offenses. The play execution begins with the quarterback attempting to false-key the defense, with a 45 degree front-out step toward his backside running-back, before pivoting on his drag foot to make a forward hand-off to the dive man (See Diagram 10-5). Then the quarterback carries out his play-side fake of an option, to discourage pursuit from the outside. The dive man is instructed to begin the play with a 45 degree jab-step toward the inside, before elevating his near elbow for the ball reception. As he receives the ball at a 2 to 2½ yard depth in the backfield, he should drive for the inside leg of his play-side guard, and break for daylight inside or outside the guard's block. The swing man takes a forward jab-step toward his onside guard during the quarterback's step-and-pivot movement, before making a counter step toward the play-side to achieve a pitch relationship on a fake option. Base blocking is suitable throughout the line, but a play-side Y-block can be used to advantage (Refer to Diagram 10-6).

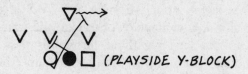

Diagram 10-6

The Counter Option replaces the Isolate Option from the Slot-I, and is used to complement the Counter Dive. The play mechanics of the Counter Dive and Counter Option are the same, basically, with the exception of the dive man who is assigned to fake a hand-off reception with an accentuated drop of his near shoulder, and then break to the outside of his guard to seal off pursuit from the backside (See Diagram 10-7). After completion of the hand-off fake to the dive man, the quarterback proceeds to attack the inside shoulder of his outside defender with a keep-or-pitch option. As the swing man acquires a fundamental pitch relationship with his quarterback, he must be ready to receive an early option-pitch in case his quarterback is confronted by a crashing end. Base-rule cut-off blocking is used at all positions along the offensive line.

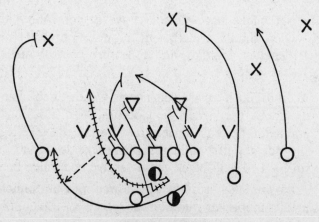

Diagram 10-7

BACK-PEDAL PASS PROTECTION
(Usable with All Keystone Patterns)

The back-pedal method of pass releasing serves as a substitute for the Slot-I's pull-up style of passing, without affecting the structure of the pass patterns. A back-pedal pocket is a natural partner to the option attack from a Slot-Veer alignment. The quarterback has the advantage of observing the immediate defensive reaction to his set-up without losing his pass pattern concentration, and also has an opportunity to "dump" the ball quickly to an alert slot back—as a "hot" receiver—when a linebacker blitz is detected (See Diagram 10-8). The linemen have an advantage of desirable inside-out blocking angles on the defensive linemen,

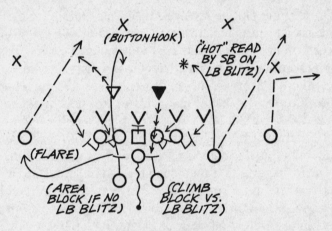

Diagram 10-8

while the set backs have flexible ways of controlling the linebackers—where there is usually a match-up in physical size. In the back-pedal pocket diagram, the following control methods are indicated:

(1) A climb block, as used against an onside linebacker blitz; if no linebacker penetration occurs, area blocking is then applied. The center blocks man "over"; if N/T, he protects slot side gap first and checks his backside second (frees the fullback to help block the defensive end when needed).

(2) An assimilated area block, followed by a buttonhook route in the linebacker middle-zone (receiver turns opposite the location of linebacker).

(3) A Flare route, after checking out a linebacker blitz. Flare control is helpful in combating a reckless charge by the onside defensive end.

(4) A combination of any two of the above is feasible in a game plan for the split-backs.

Note: an explanation of the back-pedal's organization appears in Chapter 8. Illustrations of inside-out blocking assignments for the linemen are indicated below, against Split-4 and 4-3 defenses (Diagrams 10-9 and 10-10).

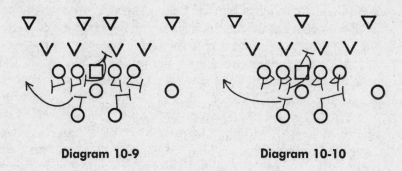

Diagram 10-9   Diagram 10-10

PLAYS MODIFIED

Modifications and Adjustments: (Diagram 10-11) 1 (2) DRAW

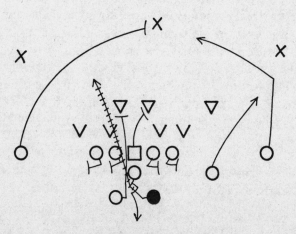

Diagram 10-11

The Draw play from the Slot-I has been modified to complement a back-pedal style of passing attack, which makes it possible to run the play to either side of the center. Its modified blocking assignments at the play-side are consistent with the blocking principles of a cup protection pocket, giving an inside-out blocking relationship on the defensive linemen. This advantage is made possible by assigning the responsibility of blocking the onside linebacker to the set back at the play-side. The backside assignments of the Draw play, however, need not be altered from those of the Slot-I. The backside guard and tackle's standard instructions are to take an inside squeeze, and, with the center, to hook their rushing linemen and/or a blitzing linebacker away from the attack hole. If a linebacker covers the center, the backside guard or the tackle and a blitz does not occur, the free blocker is instructed to protect his rush lane for two counts, permit the linebacker to drop off into his pass coverage zone, and then go after him with a cut-off block. In the backfield, the set back at the play-side should begin with a slide step inside, and observe the onside linebacker. If the onside linebacker should blitz, he must be blocked immediately to the outside. If the linebacker should hang or retreat into his pass-coverage zone, the set back then delays for two counts before going after him with a forceful climb block. The quarterback, meanwhile, should attempt to intimidate the defense into reading "pass" during his back-pedalling movement. With the quarterback's left-right-left footwork sequence, a hand-off to his right side would necessitate a pivot on his third step (left foot), before turning his trunk to make a ball exchange to his waiting runner. For a hand-off to the quarterback's left side, his number of steps should be increased to four, so that he can pivot on his right foot before turning to hand off the ball. The designated ball carrier should begin with an inside step and a delayed raise of his inside elbow, to attain proper body position and timing for the hand-off. As the ball is brought to him for the hand-off, the runner should watch the line blocking unfold at the far side of center, then follow his lead blocker through the play hole.

Modifications and Adjustments: (Diagram 10-12). BACK PEDAL PASS, SCREEN LEFT (RIGHT)

(1) *Runner (screen receiver):* Step for the onside linebacker and check for a blitz. Hold the blocking position for 2 full counts; release with the onside linemen and set up to the rear of the wall,

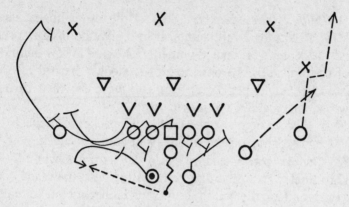

Diagram 10-12

two yards behind the line of scrimmage. Time the sequence to catch the football while in movement.

(2) *Backside back:* Step for the onside linebacker and check for a blitz. If none, drift toward the defensive end and area block.

(3) *Quarterback:* Execute back-pedal footwork while looking straight upfield. Pull-up on the fourth time-beat, then fade back two more yards and release a direct, but soft (lob), pass. Note that a screen call can be made toward or away from the formation strength, as from the Slot-I.

Significant Adjustments: (Diagram 10-13) BACK PEDAL PASS, SCREEN MIDDLE

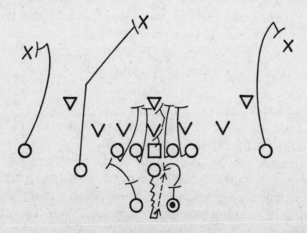

Diagram 10-13

(1) *Tailback (screen receiver):* Step for the onside linebacker and check for a blitz for 2 full counts, before pivoting inside to set up behind the center's original alignment (take care to stay behind the line of scrimmage). As from the Slot-I, "look" the ball into your hands, yell "ball" upon completion of the pass, then turn and follow patiently behind the moving wall.

(2) *Fullback:* Step for the onside linebacker and check for a blitz. If none, drift into the middle wall and area block.

(3) *Quarterback:* Execute back-pedal footwork while looking straight upfield. Pull-up on the fourth time-beat, then fade back 2 more yards and lob the ball to the waiting tailback. Note: other than the back-pedal pocket maneuver in the backfield, the fundmental execution of the Screen Middle remains the same.

Modification and Adjustments: (Diagram 10-14) 18 (17) WAGGLE
PASS

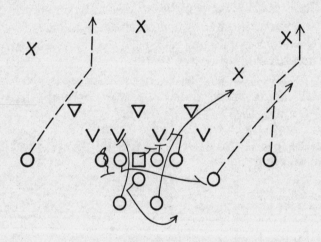

Diagram 10-14

(1) *Tight guard:* Pull from the line and assume blocking responsibility on the farside defensive end.

(2) *Quarterback and Set Backs:* Assignments are unchanged from the Slot-I, but the angles involved with the quarterback's faking, the tailback's blocking and the fullback's route release are slightly different from a split-back alignment. Note that a quarterback number (18 or 17) is indicated on a Waggle call to the slot side.

PLAYS RETAINED

Significant Adjustments: (Diagram 10-15) 2 (1) QUICK TRAP

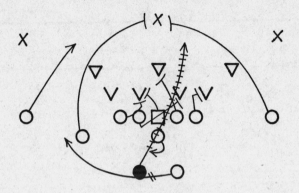

Diagram 10-15

(1) *Runner:* Angle straight for the trap hole at the farside of the center, receive the hand-off in front of the quarterback and break off the buttocks of the trapping guard as the trap block is made.

(2) *Quarterback:* Reverse-pivot in the play-side direction with a pitchback motion, as used on the Sweep play. Gain depth and complete a three-quarter spin, giving the runner his necessary space to pass in front and receive the hand-off behind the center. This spin-and-handback ball exchange will enhance the crossing action of the split-backs.

Significant Adjustments: 22 (21) TACKLE TRAP

None. Note the need to align the slot back to the short-field side, to justify his conservative, one-yard spacing (See Diagram 10-16).

Significant Adjustments: (Diagram 10-17) 2 (1) BASE

(1) *Runner:* Drive straight for the buttocks of the onside guard, receive the hand-off and then break inside, seeking the best angle for the cutback.

(2) *Quarterback:* Take a front-out step away from the scrimmage line and execute the hand-off, leaving ample room for the runner to break inside. Carry out the option fake with the backside back as he swings toward the play-side corner.

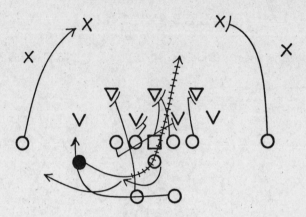

Diagram 10-16

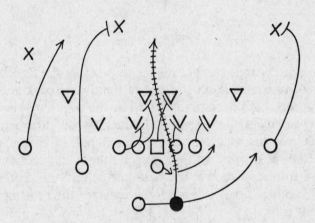

Diagram 10-17

Significant Adjustments: (Diagram 10-18) 4 (3) CROSS TRAP

(1) *Open (tight) End:* Block acrossfield on the near safety when aligned at play-side.

(2) *Runner:* Take an inside step as a delay measure during the quarterback's play-fake to the play-side set back. Then cross behind the quarterback for the ball exchange, follow behind the path of pulling guard, and drive through the farside guard-tackle trap hole.

(3) *Play-side back:* Drive straight for the backside center-guard gap, drop your inside shoulder during the hand-off fake, and fill-block for the pulling guard.

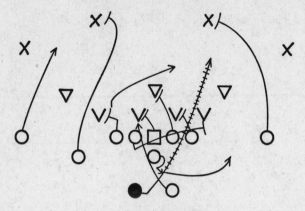

Diagram 10-18

(4) *Quarterback:* Reverse pivot in the direction of play-side—placing your back to line of scrimmage—and fake a hand-off to the play-side set back (first man across). Then complete the hand-off to the runner as he approaches from the backside (second man across). Carry out the fake of a keeper around the end.

Significant Adjustments: (Diagram 10-19) 15 (16) **LEAD OPTION**

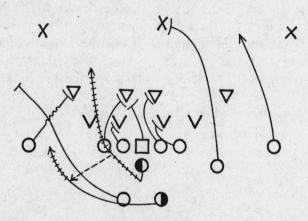

Diagram 10-19

(1) *Runner (pitch man):* Open step toward the play-side corner—eliminating the hitch step—and swing into an option-pitch relationship with the quarterback. Note that the role of the fullback and the tailback from the Slot-I are switched when the play is run to the open (tight) side of the Slot-Veer alignment.

Significant Adjustments: (Diagram 10-20) 5(6) TRAP

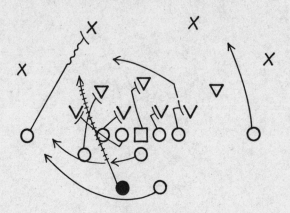

Diagram 10-20

(1) *Runner (fullback):* Drive straight for the off-tackle trap hole, eliminating bending angle in reaching the running lane. Run with force behind the trap-block of the onside guard, and concentrate on springing free during separation from the line!

(2) *Quarterback:* Front-out in full stride, angling slightly from the scrimmage line, and execute the ball exchange on the third step (if the quarterback has the sufficient length of stride). Conceal your hands on your outside hip and carry out the fake of keeper. Note the need to align the slot back to short-field side, to justify his conservative split (a necessity for off-tackle play-blocking).

Significant Adjustments: (Diagram 10-21) 7(8) SWEEP

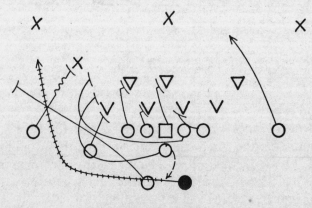

Diagram 10-21

(1) *Runner (tailback):* Expect the pitchback behind the center rather than behind the play-side tackle as from the Slot-I. Make extensive use of lead blockers, stay on the outside hip of the fullback, and use peripheral vision in searching for a cut-back opportunity whenever defensive pursuit overruns the play.

EPILOGUE

Like life itself, the challenge to succeed with a chosen football philosphy and system will face its inevitable ups and downs. There is nothing so temporary in life as success *or* failure! But for any professional to advance to the top of his or her coaching field, there must be a willingness and deep desire to acquire the background and working knowledge that will place him ahead of his competitors, without losing sight of how to draw from his many surrounding resources. For a football coach to out-achieve his competition is difficult enough in itself, but the hardest task of all is to overcome one's own subconscious impressions, which often are retained from past failings.

The game of football should teach us all to *get up instinctively when knocked to the ground!* Though this book has dealt with the ways and means to win with a proven offensive system, the whole point of playing and coaching football has been missed if deep personal pride has not been instilled, and a determined recovery of spirit after a setback has not been experienced, taught, and passed along by all who take part in this great sport. As for the fraternity of dedicated coaches, as long as we are trying to serve our God, I feel that He has a divine plan for each and every one of us.

INDEX